The Unauthorized,
Semi-Serious,
Totally Biased,
Completely Unscientific
Modern Family
as Viewed by
Uber-Fan
E. Sabbag

a.k.a.

A View of
"Modern Family"

ISBN: 0-9835506-5-4
ISBN-13: 978-0-9835506-5-5

DEDICATION

To my beloved husband Doug, who believes I can do
anything...

Contents

Acknowledgements

A big thank you to my sister, Edwina, who acted as editor for this work. Really appreciate your expertise, candor and tough love.

The cover art is a product of a talented designer, KrisMilart, whom I had the privilege to work with through 99Designs.com

This book wouldn't have been possible without the amazingly talented writers of *Modern Family*, who I hope will deliver fresh, fun, entertaining sitcoms for years to come.
Additionally, the producers of ABC who hit on a great idea and ensured it came to the small screen.

Finally, a huge thank you to my friends and family who've listened to my endless discussions of books, writing and publishing. Sadly, there are many, many more to come.

Prologue

In case you haven't guessed it, I spent time and energy to write a complete book about a sitcom because I am a HUGE fan of *Modern Family*. It's not just because the writing is sharp, funny and topical, or even because the actors are talented and bring life and energy to their roles; it's because the plotlines explore many of the social issues we encounter in the world today and these plotlines help us understand that what makes us different makes us strong. While we should strive to tolerate—even celebrate—diversity, we don't have to agree with every facet of every culture we encounter. Especially if it means that we work so hard to accept everybody else, we forget who we are. *Modern Family* is about diversity, individualism, and, most of all, family. All tied together with laughter and love.

To support the various analyses, I sprinkle in liberal doses of quotes from the series. You'll notice that I don't follow formal Modern Language Association (MLA) citation style in an effort to keep the pace dynamic. In addition, I don't indicate which episode each quote comes from. Again, I feel this would bog down the flow. If you want to learn more, I've provided the originating websites at the end of this work. In addition, if you Google any of the lines that you're interested in, you can find references to the more popular quotes on various entertainment sites. Of course, my strongest advice is to make a big bowl of popcorn, pour a glass of your favorite libation (Chardonnay, if you're a Claire or Cam fan, beer if a Phil fan, or Scotch if fond of Jay), pull up comfy chairs with your family and settle in to binge watch a marathon of *Modern Family* from the beginning. Hey, each episode runs about thirty minutes, so how long can it take? When you're done, let me know what you think — tweet @esabbagauthor #mofsabbag. I'll bet you find there's something for everyone.

1 A Family Affair

Sly & The Family Stone, 1971

A stunningly beautiful Colombian gold-digger with roots in poverty and violence. A mother of three who turns to alcohol for every situation, good or bad. A college student who resists arrest when busted for underage drinking and winds up in jail. A gay couple who adopts a Vietnamese child and then misplaces her over and over, even accidentally leaving her in a locked car and smacking her head on the ceiling. An aging businessman with a trophy wife and an ex who's prone to violent outbursts brought on by jealousy. A twelve year-old whose crush on his brother's nanny leads him to create nude drawings and sculptures. A married couple, determined to spice up their sex life celebrates Valentine's Day by meeting in a hotel bar, only to end up at the hospital when the wife collapses with a heart condition. An uber-smart teenager who lives for the day she can escape the isolation of high school by leaving for college. A real estate agent who romances lonely divorcees and single women to make deals.

Dysfunctional relationships like the ones described above create the story lines for a myriad of crime shows and dramas. These relationships could've been taken from any flavor of *Law & Order* or maybe *CSI* . Or how about decades of *Lifetime* Movies? *Dallas*? Or scores of soap opera episodes? Any or all of these stories lay the groundwork for twisted plots that can only end in tragedy. Possibly even murder or death.

However.

Not only are these *not* taken from crime shows or dramas or Florida headlines, they're recaps from one of the most popular sitcoms of the millennium – *Modern Family*. And, just in case there's somebody out there who has no social interactions or lives without electricity or access to cable or the internet (maybe they live in a treehouse or a cave or a boat or a monastery?), let's introduce the Pritchetts.

Filmed as a mockumentary, there are three overlapping social circles. But sphere indicates perfection, which doesn't adequately describe this comedic tangle. Maybe a weird oval is a better description. Or a shapeless blob. Anyway, there are three of them.

The first circle is a typical, All-American family comprised of a forty-something couple, Phil Dunphy and his wife, Claire (née Pritchett). They have three children: Haley, who is beautiful, popular, and ditzy; Alex (or Alexandria), who is nerdy, sassy, and smart; and Luke, who is goofy and his father's son all the way. Phil is a real estate agent who dreams of being an illusionist, while Claire is a stay-at-home mom who experiments with local politics, house flipping, and friending her kids on Facebook. She also never met a glass of Chardonnay that she didn't like.

The second circle is led by Claire's father, Jay Pritchett, who owns a successful closet business and lives in a house with a gated entry and a swimming pool. When he and Dede (his wife of thirty-five years) divorced, he found himself eating alone in a diner. There he heard—and fell in love with—a melodic Spanish accent. The voice actually belonged to the sister of the woman Jay marries, but Gloria, his stunningly beautiful, stunningly fiery, trophy wife, defends the deception with *"But I had to get out of that veellage..."* Their December/May romance is enlivened with Gloria's son, Manny (12 going on 45):

> **Merle:** *[after Lily knocks over a building block tower] Kids just love to destroy things.*
> **Gloria:** *Not my Manny. I would build the buildings, he would inspect them, and if they weren't up to code... ay, ay, ay, the paperwork.*

The rest of the household is comprised of Jay's cute-ugly French bulldog Stella, and the surprise baby, Fulgencio Joseph (Joe). Originally, the boy's name was Fulgencio Umberto, after Gloria's relatives, but Jay steps in. Saddling a child with the initials *FU* isn't good for anybody. Joe works just fine.

The third circle is the Tucker-Pritchett family—Mitchell (Claire's brother and Jay's son), Cameron (Mitchell's Missouri-bred, corn-fed partner), their adopted Vietnamese daughter, Lily, and Larry, the cat. Even though she's only four, Lily is scary-mature, as evidenced when she asks Haley and Alex when they're supposedly baby-sitting her, face streaked with lopsided eye makeup and lipstick, *"Is anyone watching me?"*

These are the families that interact week after week. They celebrate all things family, but that's not all. They also delve into cultural differences and what brings human beings together in love. There are stereotypes that are exaggerated to the point of farce, and there are times when the stereotypes are broken in sweet and surprising ways. The interactions are farcical, cringe-able, and even poignant, but they always evoke laughter and bring viewers back again and again and again. A major question is, why?

Sometimes it's because *"There but for the grace of God go I,"* and sometimes it's because the Pritchetts, the Dunphys, the Tucker-Pritchetts, their friends and families, and frenemies are *us*.

Enough jibber jabber. On with the show!

2 Upside Down

Diana Ross, 1980

Television shows are designed to achieve various goals: to enlighten, to motivate, to entertain. The primary goal of a farce is to entertain. This is done through improbable plot twists, fast-paced comedic interchanges and physical humor. The best way to enjoy a farce is not to try to understand or reach a deeper meaning, but to entertain the viewer with what's offered, especially when its plot is twisted into the opposite of our real-life expectations. One common expectation is that adults are adults and children are children. Obvious, simple, and hilarious when the expectation is turned upside down.

The most mature characters in *Modern Family* are the children. Manny, at age 12 and dressed in a red velvet smoking jacket, prepares a candle-lit dinner for his latest crush. *"I may not be the tallest or the most athletic, but someday I'll be the richest which is good because the ladies love that. And I've grown accustomed to a certain lifestyle."* Jay worries about Manny not being tough enough and tries to encourage his stepson to be manlier. What Jay doesn't realize is that some of Manny's behavior is due to sensitivity to Jay's insecurities. When playing chess with Jay, Manny chooses to lose. This is to avoid a temper tantrum from Jay.

Manny knows how to work his stepfather, and, in spite of Jay's strong personality, Manny remains Manny:

Manny: *Stop the car!*
Gloria: *Where you going? [Manny runs out of the car] See. You hurt his feelings.*
Jay: *Aw... well if it toughens him up a little bit then...[notices Manny] Oh, geez, he's picking flowers!*

There are other situations where Manny gets the best of Jay, without the older man having a clue. When Manny has to sell wrapping paper as a fundraiser for school, Jay is determined to teach him how a real businessman/salesman gets it done. Jay pushes the young boy to keep at it even when doors are slammed in his face, and encourages Manny to write down and remember the nuggets of wisdom Jay has learned from years of business dealings. Which Manny does. Ostensibly:

Jay: *So I'm pushing him hard; I'm an older dad, I'm not always going to be around to take care of him*
[Later...]
Manny: *You'll never go broke playing to a rich man's ego. Write that down...*

Until Joe surprises the families with his appearance, Lily is the youngest. Adopted by Cam and Mitchell from Vietnam, she directs the household more than her two dads combined do. All toddler – she bites, giggles out 'F*bleep*k" because it makes her daddy laugh, and experiments with makeup in a *Batman*'s Joker kind of way— she still manages to keep the household on an even keel. After a memorable party where Mitchell proves he *is* fun, but drinks to the point of not remembering just how <u>much</u> fun, the guys discover Dylan, Haley's ex-boyfriend, living in their spare room, and Larry the Cat dyed pink. As Dylan rambles on and on about how grateful he is to have a place to live and writes a song about a tiny pink panther, Cam and Mitchell try to determine who has to kick him out. Enter Lily. *"You can't live here, get out! It's weird, you're a big boy."* Problem solved. Now, the dads just have to figure out what to do about the biting and the cussing, and how to get Larry white again.

The Dunphy children are consistently portrayed as typical kids, but there are cracks here and there. Cam mistakenly gives Lily a $100 bill as the tooth fairy, and Haley intervenes to get the money back. On New Year's Eve, while babysitting Luke, Manny and Lily, Haley – ever the wild child – kicks a girl out of Luke's room. *"You hate me now, but someday you'll thank me! [closes door behind her] I think I owe Mom a huge apology!"* Another peek into Haley's psyche occurs when Phil and Claire take her to dinner to discuss her goals and ambitions. The parents get drunk and Haley has to drive them home, after informing them she has a successful fashion blog with tons of followers. Scatterbrained most of the time, Haley's the character with the best handle on how to navigate the social scene, virtual and real.

The youngest Dunphy, Luke, gets his head caught in the stair bannisters and mixes popcorn into pancake batter to produce self-flipping pancakes. Vacuous and fun, he reveals a devious, manipulative side at times. When Claire stresses over her mother, Dede, coming to visit, Luke volunteers to help by acting cute:

> **Phil:** *Luke, if your mom starts to lose it, I need you to act extra cute.*
>
> **Luke:** *No problem. I've got some stuff prepared. 'Hey mom, I'm firsty...' Eh? Adorable, right?...Don't worry, it works better in my jammies.*

When Manny becomes insecure about the arrival of a baby brother, Luke makes it worse...

Luke [*to the camera*]: *Sometimes, I just like to toss a grenade and run away.*

Claire and Phil worry about Luke when the boy's friend, their crotchety old neighbor Mr. Kleezak, dies. Luke doesn't react the way Claire thinks he should, and she pushes him to express grief. This is in spite of the fact that she grins every time she mentions Mr. Kleezak's passing. Luke handles his grief by taking a television that he'd been promised and Claire comes across like a maniacal reaper.

The third Dunphy child is Alex, the stereotypical nerdish, over-achieving "old person in a child's body." She plays the cello, wears glasses, has straight, brown hair and cracks under the pressure of trying to succeed.

Alex: *It's junior year, I have to get good grades. Don't you know how competitive it is out there? Stop pressuring me!*
Haley: *You know, this is what happens to kids when they're not sexually active.*

Aware that Haley is more popular and fashion forward, Alex holds her own. "*You have your fans, I have mine. One day, your fans will be working for my fans.*"

While the children act like adults, the adults are big kids. One of Cam's greatest pleasures is his alter-ego, Fisbo the clown. Mitchell doesn't understand the fascination, but goes along to make Cam happy. Seemingly, the straitlaced half of the partnership, Mitchell, is the one who shinnies down a drain pipe in a Spider Man costume after accidentally dropping his business suit into the toilet. Claire and Phil, the *Modern Family* version of Ozzie and Harriet, fill their pockets with candy and water so they don't have to pay for snacks at the movie theater.

Phil: *I brought my own snacks, not because I'm cheap; it's a matter of principle. Plus, I get a little rush from the danger. Be cool, be cool, be cool! Just look straight ahead... I've never felt more alive. Woo-hoo!*

While on their way into *Croctopus*, a sci-fi schlock fest about a mutant cross between a crocodile and an octopus, they run into another couple of parents who have a child in Alex's class who is the only one smarter than Alex. Competition gets the better of her, and Claire follows them into a socially significant foreign film, where she falls asleep within minutes. Catching up with Phil afterwards, still wearing his 3D glasses, Claire's told *"It was a female – and pregnant!"*

Eyes wide and in a breathless whisper, *"Croctopi!"*

And then there's Jay, the patriarch of the clan, a Scotch-swilling, set-in-his-ways, golfing capitalist who doesn't tolerate emotion or signs of physical affection and is all adult. Most of the time. Sometimes, he's the babiest of the babies.

Manny: *I wish I could stay home with you and fly toy airplanes.*

Jay: *These aren't toy airplanes, Manny, these are models and they're very complicated. You wanna fly one of these you gotta be familiar with air foil, drag, lift and these are all principles of aerodynamics.*

Manny: *The box says 12 and up.*

Jay: *[Staring at the box] What!?*

Gloria: *You can fly toy planes with Jay next time. Today you are going to spend time with Luke.*

Manny: *Why?*

Gloria: *Because his mother invited you so you go. Family needs to be close, right Jay?*

Jay: *[Mumbling to himself] I'm pretty sure that's a typo.*

While Jay's normally the strongest male figure in the family, he pales when compared to Gloria's ex-husband, Javier. Jay confronts Gloria with how she and Manny could be taken in by such a shallow, self-absorbed person – a person who promises to visit his son and then cops out at the last minute, leaving Manny waiting on a curb for a father who never shows. Gloria tries to explain.

Jay: *Manny thinks his dad is like superman. Truth: he's a total flake. In fact, the only way he's like superman is that they both landed in this country illegally.*

Gloria: *Manny's very passionate. Just like his father. My first husband: very handsome but too crazy. It seem like all we did was fight and make love. Fight and make love. Fight and make love. One time, I'm not kidding you, we fell out the window together.*

Jay: *[Uneasy chuckle] [To Gloria] Which one were you doing? [To camera crew] I'm hearing this for the first time.*

To prove their admiration and love are misplaced, Jay intercepts Javier when he comes to visit Manny. The two men play pool and begin talking about baseball. Javier takes Manny and Jay to Dodger Stadium to hit baseballs and later promises Jay he'll introduce him to some baseball players at the bar. Jay falls asleep and, the next day, waits eagerly on the curb for Javier to come get him. Hours later, Javier still hasn't arrived. Gloria and Manny gather up a dejected Jay and lead him into the house, arms wrapped around him in consolation.

Upside down indeed.

3 Love is in the Air

Tom Jones, 1979

Some Internet chatter focuses on the lack of physical interactions between romantically involved characters on *Modern Family,* specifically between Cameron and Mitchell. LGBT (Lesbian Gay Bisexual Transgender – if ever an acronym is called for, this is the time) advocates are concerned that the network is shying away from presenting gay intimacy, evidenced by the fact that the same sex couple rarely kiss, hug or otherwise display their physical attraction to each other.

Here's a thought.

Consider how many times the other couples engage in any form of display of affections, public or private. Gloria and Jay – rarely, if ever, hug or kiss. It makes one wonder how she got pregnant! Especially when Jay uses Manny to strategically interrupt them when it becomes clear that Gloria wants action. As for Claire and Phil, their rendezvous are interrupted by their children, Claire's heart giving out, and nude hot tub aficionados on New Year's Eve.

The truth of the genre is that sensitive, sexy,

provocative scenes of intimacy aren't that funny. This is a sitcom. A farce. It exists for laughs with hints of poignancy, not the other way around. And that's okay. Other sitcoms handle public displays of affection in the same manner. On *The Big Bang Theory*, Leonard and Penny have kissed—maybe—a half dozen times throughout seven seasons. Ditto for Howard and Bernadette. Amy and Sheldon have kissed twice and Rajeesh doesn't have a girlfriend. But, in the words of Kelly on *Married with Children* – "I digest…" The series is rife with crushes, love and romance, *Modern Family* style.

The most dysfunctional relationship in the series is the most traditional – Claire and Phil. They have the two-story house in the suburbs, three happy, well-adjusted children, satisfying careers and an active social life. They role play by meeting in a hotel bar and plan romantic get-aways – even renewing their wedding vows in Hawaii. Norman Rockwell all the way (on the outside). Their actions paint a more Dali-esque or Picasso-like portrait.

Phil obsesses over Gloria, which Claire tolerates with a twisted expression and a glass of Chardonnay.

[About Gloria and Claire]
Phil: *I just hate it when my two girls fight.*
Claire: *How exactly is she your girl?*

Phil: *Gloria, we all know you'd be fine without underwear.*

Luke: *Eww, gross. I didn't know grandpa could still do it.*
Phil: *Don't be disrespectful, Luke! Anyone could do it with Gloria.*

Phil: *Am I attracted to her? Yes! Would I ever act on it? No! No way. Not while my wife is still alive.*

Before feeling sorry for Claire, one has to examine her

behavior in the relationship. While Phil writhes in agony from an undiagnosed pain in his side, Claire gets dressed up for the sexy firemen that she knows will answer her daughters' 911 call. The behavior is compounded when Claire discourages Phil from accompanying her to her college reunion. Claire wants to go alone to uncover "*what if*" as it pertains to a sexy professor she had a torrid affair with. When Phil surprises her by showing up anyway, they both attend a party at the professor's apartment, where Claire answers "*what if*" by observing the harpy that is the professor's wife – a harpy that was originally excited and in love and content until brought down by the professor's juvenile, party boy ways. Again, the upside-down theme bobs into play and Claire realizes that her life isn't so bad after all.

It's never completely clear whether Claire is happy or not with her decision to marry Phil. When the couple attends a counseling session with Luke, Claire reveals that she's concerned Luke will grow up to be like his father – irresponsible and goofy forever. While fighting about this revelation, they each leave in separate cars and forget Luke in the parking lot. Ever resourceful, Luke arrives triumphantly in a limo while they're scrambling to find him. Claire's insistence that Haley break up with her boyfriend, Dylan, may be rooted in the fact that Dylan could be a younger Phil, especially as Phil's obsession with Dylan borders on a bromance – possibly seeing himself in the teenager and really liking what he sees.

But with all these questions, there are glimmers of the love they have for each other. While shopping with Gloria, Phil sees an old high school classmate—a rival that he never felt he was able to best—and makes it appear that Gloria is his wife. The classmate comments that he was always jealous of Phil:

Phil: *Jealous of me? Why?*
Classmate: *Always figured you'd wind up with Claire*

Pritchett. *God, was she beautiful.*
Phil: *Claire?*
Classmate: *Sure.   Silky blonde hair.   Beautiful brown eyes.   Whoever wound up with her was one lucky son of a bitch.*

From that point on, Phil pushes Gloria aside to ensure Claire knows how much he loves her and wants her. Juvenile, true, that Phil only seems to want Claire when someone else sees her as desirable, but for this episode at least, Phil is once again enamored of Claire. Then Claire shows her love for him, in her own way.

On the first day of school, Claire looks forward to the first day all to herself; she plans to run, read and just generally relax., but Phil is clinging to her and challenges her to a race:

Claire: *Getting everybody out of the house in the morning can be really tough. Especially the first day of school.*
Phil: *From the moment we get up at seven until we drop them off at school it is: go go go.*
Claire: *I get up at six.*
Phil *[mocking]*: *I get up at five.*
Claire: *Seriously, I get up at six.*
Phil: *That's you? I thought we had a raccoon.*

Claire: *Phil, let it go, I'm faster than you*
Phil: *If only there was some way we could settle this once and for all, but how?*
Claire: *You seriously want to race me? I ran a half-marathon last year*
Phil: *Okay, I'm half scared*
Claire: *Okay, we do need to do this. I'll go change*

As predicted, Claire is trouncing Phil, when she realizes that he's struggling with the children going off to school. Since she considers him her biggest child, she lets him win.

Now that's love.

It's not always just about the children, or being children. Sometimes, Phil and Claire go the extra mile to rekindle the smoldering flames of romance, or at least the enduring sizzle of Clive Bixby and Julianna. Clive is Phil's alternate personality – a traveling salesman who picks up hot women in hotel bars. Julianna is Claire's contribution, a hot woman in a hotel bar. They introduce these characters (the couple is reprised throughout the series) on Valentine's Day when Phil tries to outdo Dylan's gift of a photo turned portrait of him and Haley. To compete, Phil whisks Claire off to a fancy hotel and convinces her to do some role-playing. Julianna/Claire is drinking at the bar, alone, when Clive/Phil walks up:

> **Clive/Phil:** *I design high-end electroacoustic transducers.*
> **Julianna/Claire:** *Wow, that is very...specific.*
> **Clive:** *That's just a fancy way of saying I get things to make noise. (Damn, that was a good one.)*

> After stumbling slightly by complaining that his wife is always tired, Clive/Phil scores again:
> **Julianna/Claire:** *So if your wife is so beautiful, what are you doing here with me?*
> **Clive/Phil:** *Because I respect her too much to do the things I want to do to you tonight.*
> **Julianna/Claire:** *[rowlll...] Jackpot.*

Claire excuses herself and returns to the bar dressed in a trench coat, as it turns out, ONLY in a trench coat. Which is daring and exciting and romantic, right up until she gets the belt caught in an escalator and people they know stop to try to help. The help mostly consists of suggestions that she just take the coat off. At least Phil hits the EMERGENCY STOP button, which stops the escalator from ripping the coat off her. This leaves Claire vulnerable and without much hope until Gloria and Jay walk up, fresh from their Valentine's date. Gloria and Jay assess the situation—very correctly. Jay is disgusted and Gloria is sympathetic—*We've all been there.*

Acting quickly, Gloria wraps her coat around Claire and acts as a shield while Claire wiggles out of her traitorous garment. Phil is entranced by the maneuver and wants to continue in character, but Claire shuts him down by dropping her black thong panties in front of her dad as she scurries away. A couple has to be in love to survive a humiliation like that.

And then there's Haley. There are allusions throughout that she's sexually active, but she's never caught in a compromising position nor engaged in physical intimacy. The closest this comes is one of the numerous times Dylan is seen climbing out a window and found sleeping on the sofa or sneaking down the stairs. The best instance of the second example is Dylan getting trapped inside the house when the family leaves for a vacation in Hawaii. The alarm screeches as he escapes down the sidewalk. Eventually, whether through Claire's intervention or because Haley is growing up, Haley breaks up with Dylan and shows interest in a nerdy, goofy young man, Andy, who takes care of Joe, Jay and Gloria's baby. When Alex points out that Andy is remarkably similar to Phil, Haley freaks out. Luckily, Claire isn't around to witness this or the subsequent re-enactment of *Gravity* by Phil and Andy. Nobody should've witnessed that.

Of course, the 300-lb. gorilla in the room is Cam and Mitchell's relationship. Given that it's *Modern Family*, there is an actual 300-lb. gorilla—albeit stuffed—sitting in the living room along with an elephant.

> **Mitchell:** *This is ridiculous; we need to talk about the elephant in the room.*
> *[Pause. Pan to a huge stuffed elephant in the corner]*

Cam [*to the camera*]: *The giant stuffed elephant was a gift from our good friend Pepper.*
Mitchell: *Gay guys having kids is relatively new, so our community has not yet learned how to modulate baby gifts.*
Cam: *When Steven and Stephan had little Rocko, our friend Longinus sent over the entire cast of "Yo Gabba Gabba."*
Mitchell: *Now Rocko cries whenever he sees bright colors.*
Cam: *I'm not allowed over there.*

Passionate love scenes slow down the energy of a well-written sitcom. For *Modern Family*, the choice is to concentrate on the family aspects of the various relationships to show intimacy and love. When a rude driver bumps into Mitchell at a gas station, Cam, resplendent in clown makeup and dress, forces the redneck to apologize to *"my boyfriend."*

Cam: *I'm the ass kicking clown that will twist you like a balloon animal!*

Mitchell smiles a tiny happy smile after Cam produces a giant alarm clock from his clown jacket and says, *"C'mon, we're going to be late."* But their life isn't all sight gags and slapstick. When Mitchell spends a day trapped in a treehouse with Claire, it reminds him how lucky he is to have had a sister. He tells Cam he wants to have another child and Cam suggests a boy. For various reasons, traditional channels fail and they decide to expand their family by adopting a child from Mexico. When the surrogate mother is ready to give birth, a road trip ensues with Gloria in tow since she speaks Spanish. The resulting birth scene emulates a *Telemundo* soap opera, with Gloria translating and adding to the debacle. In the end, the birth mother keeps the baby, Cam and Mitchell are devastated, and Gloria reveals she's pregnant.

Sobbing in a barren, weed-strewn lot, a heart-broken Mitchell is comforted by Cam. More than a steamy embrace or a fervent make-out session, this poignant scene where the two men break down and decide to give up on what seems to be a fruitless quest for another child exemplifies the love they have for each other.

At this point, the proud, self-assured Gloria reveals her insecurity. She's terrified that Jay will be angry when he finds out she's pregnant. It's obvious that it's not his money she's concerned about, but the home and the sense of family that they've created together. Manny increases her concerns when he expresses doubts about her ability to raise a child.

> **Gloria** *[telling Manny that she's pregnant]: This is not your responsibility.*
> **Manny:** *Neither is a wooden salad bowl, but I'm the only who oils it.*
> **Gloria:** *Manny, I can take care of a baby. I took care of you.*
> **Manny:** *Please. I was an anomaly. I self-potty-trained.*

Her fears are baseless, as Jay professes that he's excited about the opportunity to try again and be a better father and husband, until Dede appears on the scene. Remember the crazy, jealous ex-wife? Jay tries to keep Gloria's pregnancy from the ex-wife, but she finds out on a surprise visit. Also surprising is that she's thrilled, to the point of hysteria, to discover that Gloria's expecting. It's not that surprising when Dede exploits the situation by pointing out that Jay was an absent dad and she replants seeds of doubt. Once Dede leaves, Jay reassures Gloria that he couldn't be happier. Now that the business is thriving and he doesn't have to be there every day, he can help more at home and be more engaged with their child:

> **Jay:** *I don't know what happened. Maybe it's what robot*

Lincoln [automaton from Disneyland] said about a man's duty or keeping the union together. Maybe I just chickened out. But I realized that staying with my kids was more important than leaving my wife. That's not the right decision for everyone, but it was the right decision for me. So I stuck it out 'till they were grown.

Gloria: *[Off screen] Jay, come join me in the Jacuzzi!*

Jay: *And the universe rewarded me.*

Gloria: *I'm going to take a shower. Do you care to join me?*

Jay: *You know, honey, there is a gun in the footlocker in the garage. If I ever say no to that question I want you to use it on me.*

Jay: *I've always seen life like a series of doors. Sometimes you get to choose the door you go through, and sometimes you don't get that choice. But you still have to walk through it. So either you can go through kicking and screaming, or walk through with your head held high. And since I don't get to choose the door I'm about to go through, I just pray it's a healthy, happy kid. And a boy.*

Having the baby brings Jay and Gloria closer, but Jay has no delusions about their relationship or the potential problems their age difference may bring. He even attempts to learn salsa steps from Manny because Gloria loves to dance:

Manny: *You're dancing, not invading Poland*

Mitchell: *Looking for Jay Pritchett; big man, wrestles with homophobia?*

The salsa lessons turn out well, but Jay freely confesses that there's still a generation gap between him and Gloria. He says it in so many words:

Jay: *He's been on Johnny Carson a hundred times.*
Gloria: *Who's Johnny Carson?*

Jay: *[to the camera] Is there a generation gap? Sure. Sometimes it causes problems. She thought Simon and Garfunkel were my lawyers.*

Maybe Jay should croon *Bridge Over Troubled Waters* to Gloria. Now that would bridge the gap. Or make it wider. Either way, it would make for an interesting plot twist.

4 Surprise, Surprise

Bruce Springsteen 2009

Stereotypes can be funny. They're predictable and it's obvious when to laugh - Gloria's obsession with shoes; Cam, in full costume from a community theater presentation of *Cats,* staging a sit-in protesting a tree in a neighborhood park that's about to be cut down. Liberal. Theatrical. Gay. Haley, a teenager, savvy in all things social media and life as a whole, while Phil is the antithesis without having a clue that he's clueless. Or maybe he does:

> **Phil:** *I'm a cool dad, that's my thing. I'm hip, I surf the web, I text. LOL means laugh out loud, OMG: oh my god, WTF: why the face.*

> **Phil:** *A Realtor's just a ninja in a blazer. The average burglar breaks in and leaves clues everywhere. But not me; I'm completely clueless.*

Manny and his love of poetry, cooking and velvet smoking jackets; Haley is beautiful and dumb; Alex is serious and smart. There have been variations on these themes over the years, in countless other sitcoms and the audience enjoys them.

But.

There have been variations on these themes over the years, in countless other sitcoms, and the audience tires of them. The laughs stop. A smart, clever sitcom with smart clever writers succeeds because they keep the laughs coming. *Modern Family* is smart and clever, and the writers know when to break the stereotypes.

Surprise!

Phil is one of the most predictable characters. He appears to be less than intelligent, especially when compared to his daughter, Alex:

> **Alex:** *I can't believe it. I got a "B" on my paper.*
> **Phil:** *Good for you.*
> **Claire:** *Yeah.*
> **Alex:** *No, it would be good for you. It's terrible for me. Thanks to your moldy encyclopedias, my take on mitosis was completely out of date. They don't even call it "protoplasm" anymore. It's "cytoplasm".*
> **Claire:** *Well, you could have asked one of us.*
> **Alex:** *Now you're making jokes?*
> **Claire:** *I'm not making a joke.*
> **Alex:** *Really? What's the difference between a gamete and a zygote?*
> *[Claire is at a loss for words]*
> **Phil:** *Don't fall for it, Claire. She's just making up words.*

> **Phil:** *In nature, fathers are known to eat their young. Is it because they are delicious? No. It's because they want to give their female: bear, giraffe, what have you – the honeymoon they never had. Just to be clear I'm not condoning eating your kids, but I sure as heck don't mind if giraffes do it.*

Phil fantasizes about the "perfect" birthday gift—the

latest iPad—but knows that Claire will fail to get it for him. He dreams about Gloria and accidentally flirts with single mothers and real estate clients. He takes pride in being a friend to his children as opposed to being a father, a mean guy. He always seems to come in second, or third or fourth to the other real estate agents in the area. He provides the main income to the family, seemingly a nice one, but is the constant brunt of jokes and a source of derision.

And this gets old, even cringeable, especially when Phil is out-maneuvered again and again by his arch rival, Gil Thorpe—a rival who hires Claire to work in his office and overshadows Phil on Luke's career day. Phil admires Gil to the point of hero worship, constantly getting swamped in Gil's wake:

> **Phil:** *[at career day] Gil Pickles. Genius! Much better than my Phil-low Cases.*

> **Phil:** *This house is going to sell. Because who's the best realtor in town?*
> **Claire:** *Gil Thorpe.*
> **Phil:** *That's right, and he's bringing potential buyers tomorrow.*

Just when the audience is on the verge of crying *"Enough!"*, Phil has enough. In the episode *Fulgencio*, Claire is too busy helping Gloria with the baby's baptism to handle the family's problems. Phil steps in and convinces Haley, Alex and Luke to handle the situations with kindness. When the kids baulk, Phil intervenes for them:

> **Phil:** *And then I realized, my kids didn't understand the concept of killing with kindness, because they've never seen it. So I'm going to show them, by going on a hugicidal rampage.*

This makes each situation much, much worse – to the point of where the children feel they can't be seen in public ever again. This pushes Phil to a breaking point where he channels Michael Corleone with Luke acting as his hit man. Thus follows a revenge rampage, complete with placing the head of a toy-stuffed zebra in the bed of one of Luke's classmates:

> **Claire:** *Isn't it crazy how all our kids' problems just disappeared?*
> **Phil:** *Don't ever ask me about my business, Claire.*

In recent years, there's been a trend towards sitcom couples comprised of a smart, successful, beautiful woman paired with a bumbling, laughable man that everyone tolerates more than respects or likes. Back to a previous comment, originally this was funny and fresh, but this concept has been overused to the point of being extremely stale. Claire is smart and beautiful, successful as a stay-at-home mom, while Phil is the bumbling, laughable man. Ho-hum...

One break in this repetitious plot line is the *Godfather* spoof. Another is the sprinkling of Phil's successes in the real estate market – winning a prestigious award or selling a house to Mitchell's boss just hours before going the first month in years without a sale. The best, by far, is when Gil Thorpe stops by the house after the sons clash in a wrestling match. Gil's son was the victor, followed by an incident at a diner where it appeared Luke attacked the other boy, but it actually turned out to be Luke applying the Heimlich maneuver. Not really, but everyone assumed that he was saving Gil's son from choking and Luke didn't correct anyone. Regardless, Gil stopped by to say "thanks and no hard feelings," whereupon he picked up Lily while Phil egged them on and even encouraged Lily to get really close and rub her had against Gil's   (mainly because Lily had contracted lice). Who says Phil is dumb?

The other major tangent from the stereotypical storyline is Claire. She's lovely, confident and appears smart, but she has her vulnerabilities. This is exemplified when she runs for town council, "officially" to get a stop sign installed on their street, but personally to make her family proud of her. When the initial reviews come in that she's behind because people find her sarcastic, mean-spirited and unlikeable, the family holds a mock debate to give her pointers on improving her image:

> **Phil:** *Honey, you're not unlikeable.*
> **Claire:** *Thank you.*
> **Phil:** *You just seem unlikeable.*

Unfortunately, the family's help makes the situation much, much worse. Claire crashes and burns in a debate with the incumbent town council member, Duane Bailey:

> **Duane:** *I can assure you, doggie suicide is real. It's just not covered by the mainstream media because it's not as sexy as feline AIDS.*

> **Jay:** *[watching Claire trying to remain composed at the debate] It's like watching the Hindenburg.*
> **Gloria:** *It's the most horrible thing I've ever seen in my life.*
> **Phil:** *[standing up] Excuse me.*
> **Jay:** *Stand by.*

> **Phil:** *I am Phil Dunphy, and I am not a pervert. I, like a lot of men in this town, enjoy making love to my wife. I mean, uh... I mean with their wives. Not me, them! Look, I should probably just sit down and say nothing, but it's too late. I am standing, and I'm obviously talking, and now you're looking at me, and I feel the need to keep going.*

This side of Claire continues to be explored throughout the series, and is magnified when she goes back into the work force. She has a series of missteps, including one very short stint working for Phil's nemesis, Gil Thorpe, before settling into her father's closet business. Even in the corporate environment, people don't really like her, but they have to put up with her because she's the boss' daughter. Successful, yes, she works hard and gets the job done, but Claire is where she is because of nepotism and not because she's all that great. Even her kids aren't quite on board with her:

Claire: *Hey how come you guys haven't accepted my friend requests?*
Haley: *I didn't know you were on Facebook.*
Alex: *Yeah you said it was only for teenagers or people who wanted to have affairs.*

As a couple, Claire is the unlikeable, stern parent, while Phil is the understanding, 'cool' dad that the kids like to hang around with, and this is good for laughs. But when they decide to switch places—actually Claire decides because she's tired of being the mean parent—it gets even better.

Phil is tasked with making Haley and Alex clean their bathroom, while Claire has the opportunity to take Manny and Luke go carting and other fun activities. By the end of the day, the girls are frazzled, starving and nauseous from cleaning hair out of the drains, and the boys are frazzled, and over-stuffed with junk food and nauseous from being forced to ride roller coasters and bumper cars too fast. During the latter, Claire runs both boys into the wall while laughing maniacally. Phil does a great Simon Legree imitation (he won an Emmy for his character in this episode) and Claire is only missing the green hair and white pancake makeup to complete her Joker portrayal:

The Ol' Switcheroo:

Phil: *But I was going to take Luke and Manny go-karting for their good report cards.*

Claire: *What was good about Luke's report card?*

Phil: *...He didn't lose it.*

The Meltdowns:

Phil: *[after Hayley and Alex trick him] You poked the bear, girls! You poked him!*

Alex: *Dad, we haven't had lunch yet.*

Phil: *Neither have half the kids in Africa. Stop yappin' and get back to work.*

Manny: *I'd like a chicken breast with no skin, please.*

Claire: *What, are you going to the ball Cinderella? Live a little.*

Luke *[to the camera]: I didn't want the milkshake either, but after what happened to Manny, I wasn't saying a thing.*

Luke: *I don't feel well.*

Claire: *Did you finish your milkshake?*

Luke: *I think that's the problem.*

Claire: *Luke, honey, come back. I said I was sorry.*

Luke: *I'm 12, I need limits.*

Phil: *They're monsters, Claire! Deceitful, manipulative monsters and they need to be broken.*

All's Well That Ends:

Phil: *[Note to Claire] If you want family drama, rent "Spy Kids." They save their parents. You think they could have done that if they got yelled at?*

Phil: *I don't like being you.*

Claire: *Nobody does.*

One final comment about the trend in portraying 'typical' white, Anglo-Saxon, Protestant, middle-American couples. Why do the hot wives wear flat shoes, nondescript khakis and untucked, cotton blouses with collars and the sleeves rolled up? Do Lois Griffin (from *Family Guy*) and Claire Dunphy shop from the same L.L. Bean catalogue?

Similar to Claire, Gloria is beautiful, confident and smart. Both are stay-at-home moms who love their children and their husbands. Both are disliked by people in the community, but for very different reasons. Claire has already been done to death, so now it's time to look at Gloria. And people do look, which is the main reason that Gloria is so disliked. She's the stereotypical Latino bombshell who lands a rich, older man to enable her to break away from the poverty-ridden life she has for herself and her son, Manny. This is another potential for a major yawn, but this plotline is saved by glimpses into Gloria's insecurities, her vulnerability and her deep love for Jay.

The insecurities are revealed in typical *Modern Family* style. After a disastrous family brunch, Claire leaves with the announcement that she's heading to yoga. Gloria asks to come along and Claire rebuffs her, but then they run into each other in a location far from the yoga studio. Realizing she's caught in a lie, Claire comes clean and admits that she's really heading to an indoor gun range to blow off steam by blowing off some rounds:

> **Claire:** *I know on the outside I look like I have everything together.*
> **Gloria:** *No, not really.*

Once inside, Gloria coolly shoots a bull's-eye and leaves. Gloria's insecurity shows by following Claire to call her out, but Gloria pulls it off in the end. However, Gloria's not so victorious when she accompanies Manny on a school field trip to the museum. Intimidated by the other mothers, Gloria is holding her own until she has an allergic reaction and her face turns bright red. She wants to sneak out the back, but Manny convinces her to stand up to the other women. At the last minute, Manny intercedes for her and distracts everyone by making a big deal of his squeaky shoes. Gloria is elegant, beautiful, sharp shooting, and willing to be protected by her twelve-year-old son. What's not to love? And Manny does love her; very, very much. Even though Latino women are supposed to be protective and nurturing of their children, Gloria falls short at times. Way, way short. Remember that Manny is self-potty-trained? It gets worse:

> **Gloria:** *No one knows this but for the first year of his life, I made up Manny like a girl and told everyone he was my daughter. [Gloria laughs; Jay looks petrified.] Ay, but just for a few times. I didn't want to mess with his head. When he found the pictures I told him it was his twin sister who died. [Jay's terrified]*

> **Gloria** *[A Mother's Day Episode]:* *I love Manny, but sometimes, I...be a boy. Go outside kick a ball and steal something.*

Of all the characters on the show, Jay is the one allowed to be the most stereotypical. Even when he cries while watching *Miracle on 34th Street*, it's in character:

> **Manny:** *Are you crying?*
> **Jay:** *What are you, a robot? It's a deeply emotional movie.*

And this is okay. Jay is the pillar of the family — the patriarch that's unchanging and unflappable. Instead of being boring or embarrassing, it gives the show a sense of stability, of structure, of home.

All of this is in direct contrast to Cameron, the misplaced country boy. Flaming, theatrical, high-pitched at times and always over the top, Cam is the quintessential gay man. He loves dressing Lily up in costumes and makeup reminiscent of old-time Hollywood glamor and rock stars, and he cries when talking about *Sophie's Choice:*

Mitchell: *Why is our daughter dressed like Donna Summer?*
Cam: *She's not Donna Summer. Clearly, she's Diana Ross from her RCA years.*

When Lily starts school and Cam suffers from empty nest syndrome, he takes on a job of music teacher at the local high school. Everything about Cam is funny, exaggerated and expected when he accepts the position of football coach and exposes his testosterone-ridden, competitive self.

What?!

Yes.

He convinces Manny to win the final game, even when playing against a team whose coach had just died:

Cam: *Tragic news about Coach Knight... But you know what? We need to focus up! Plenty of time to pay our respects, but there will be no mourning Knight this afternoon!*

But in the end, he comes through and Cam is back to being Cam.

Manny: *You think someday they might name this field after you?*
Cam: *You're not the first person to think along those lines. Earlier today, someone in the faculty bathroom was messing around with the phrase, 'Cameron Tucker Dome.'*

Being young and malleable, the children are perfect candidates for wriggling out of what's expected. The Dunphy clan maintains their personae most consistently. There are a few digressions, but not many. Alex is mostly smart, sarcastic, and somewhat nerdy-looking. She's the good girl who feels the weight of being the only one in the family with a potential for success —the one who has to make the name Dunphy mean something. Therefore, it's a complete shock to her pretty, popular sister – and the audience – when strait-laced, too-good-to-be-true Alex agrees to break into the high school with Haley and they get arrested. At the exact moment when Cam and Mitchell are trying to decide who should take care of Lily if anything happens to them. Oh, and Luke arrives in a limo because his parents forgot to bring him home after a counseling session.

ANNNKKKK!!!

Claire and Phil are out. Even though they're the traditional couple, the Dunphy's are not to be trusted with any more children.

This brings us to Luke. Dropped on his head repeatedly as a child, never seeming to be all there, Luke is an athlete and a cool kid, and he wants to help decorate sets for the school musical:

Classmate: *Why is it taking you so long? How hard is it for you to paint a wall?*

Luke: *A lot harder than your so-called singing. At least this is supposed to be flat.*

Luke: *Hey, dad, you coming to my play tonight?*

Alex: *Your play? You only painted the sets.*

Luke: *Yeah? And Michelangelo only painted the Sixteenth Chapel.*

Alex: *Maybe don't keep your face so close to the paint cans.*

Luke is dragged into the *Phantom of the Opera* when Cam loses his star and he finds out Luke has an exquisite voice. And insanity.

> **Cameron** *[on choosing Luke as an understudy]: He knows the show, he sings like a nightingale and he has a certain theatrical madness in his eyes you cannot teach.*
> **Manny:** *That's just from all the paint."*

It is a part that Manny desperately wants and, in any other sitcom, he would have gotten. The laughs could've been worked out somehow, but in *Modern Family*-land, Manny can't sing. He can write poetry, cook, and play a pan flute, but, like his mother, his voice could make a person beg for fingernails on a chalkboard. The inability to sing aside, Manny's talents predetermine that he will take after his uncles, or at the very least, make him embrace his metrosexuality and become the ultimate girly man. Except for one major discordance--he's a great football player. A major surprise in the show's relationship tangle is that Cam's best actor / singer is Luke and his best football player is Manny. Metro-Manny still reigns supreme:

> **Manny:** *If you're at the store later could you pick up some ice? I'm gonna need it for after the game.*
> **Jay:** *My little athlete...*
> **Manny:** *I want to try out the gelato maker I traded my bike for.*
> **Jay:**...*lures me in every time."*

While many tweens struggle with acceptance, Manny takes middle school in stride to the point of manipulating the cool kids:

> **Jay:** *We think that Griffin might be hanging out with you*

because he's got a little crush on your mother and me.
Gloria: *On you?*
Manny: *Wow. I can't believe it.*
Jay: *Listen, it's fine. You're gonna be fine.*
Gloria: *I'm sorry.*
Manny: *Are you kidding? It's fantastic!*
Jay: *How is it fantastic?*
Manny: *I'm only hanging out with him because I have the hots for his sister Chloe. You've met Griffin; the kid's a doorknob.*

Manny: *[on finding out that Griffin has a crush on Gloria just before a pool party] Excellent! Dress accordingly...*

5 It's A Small World After All

The Sherman Brothers, 1963

In addition to smashing stereotypes and delving into relationships, *Modern Family* also takes a poke at cultures. There are several interwoven, colliding, fantastical worlds in the form of Fiery Latino vs. White Bread America; Country vs. City; Gay vs. Hetero; Adoptive vs. Biological Offspring; and Old vs. Young. If not done properly, this can come across as bigoted, bullying and even hateful. As with all things *Modern Family,* the show is tempered with respect, panache and, of course, a healthy dose of love.

The results are everyone showing not just tolerance for the diversity in their family, but enjoying the adventure. For the most part. At other times, the cultural divisions cause colossal fireworks and meltdowns. What better time to have an emotional blowup than the holidays? Let's consider Claire's favorite holiday, Halloween (she was born on Halloween, 1974):

Claire: *I didn't complain when we had to open presents on Christmas Eve or shoot off fireworks because Gloria explained that's how they do it in Colombia. And I didn't make a scene when Cam and Mitchell took over Thanksgiving and we couldn't have a traditional turkey* *dinner any more.*

Cam: *That's a lot of complaining for somebody who asked for thirds of our tandoori turkey last year.*

Claire: *All I want is for one holiday to be mine. Just one. Halloween. Is that too much to ask?*

The episode ends with everyone coming together for Claire and making it a Halloween to remember, but the meltdown reveals the underlying tensions that each hold inside of them. This is in response to the colliding worlds mentioned before. The first to consider is the culture clash between Latin America (Colombia, specifically) and Middle/Upper Class America.

In the real world, tensions arise from immigration issues, communities with language barriers, and attempts to maintain ancestral culture. Tensions also result while assimilating new cultures, which cause debates, arguments and even legislation. On *Modern Family*, the tensions come from language confusion, struggles to maintain ancestral culture, and the jealousy that occurs when a gorgeous Latino woman and her metrosexual son are introduced into a traditional American family. Okay, *"traditional"* is used quite loosely, but it's to make a point. Gloria, with her mangled English and fiery Latino temper, is a target for well-aimed cultural barbs. Manny, a debonair ladies' man in a twelve year old body, has his own bull's-eye on his chest:

Gloria: *We're very different. Jay's from the city. He has big business. I come from a small village. Very poor but very, very beautiful. It's the number one village in all Colombia for all the... What's the word?*

Jay: *Murders.*

Gloria: *Yes, the murders.*

Gloria: *I'm Colombian, I know a fake crime scene when I see one.*

Gloria: *[commenting on Manny's desire to wear traditional Colombian garb on the first day of school and performing a native dance while playing a flute]* The poncho by itself was fine. The poncho plus the flute, plus the stupid dance; my son will die a virgin.
Jay: *That's right.*

Jay: *[standing beside the car with Gloria and Manny]* Hey sport, can I take a look at that whistle?
(Jay drops the flute but it doesn't break)
Jay: *Oh geez, look at that.*
Gloria: *And now you've stepped on it!*
Jay: *What?!*
(Jay now steps on the flute, breaking it.)
Jay: *Ugh! What's wrong with me!*

Gloria: *TAXI! You see, they don't stop because I'm Latina!*
Haley: *Or because that was just a yellow car...*

Gloria: *Oh, here we go, because in Colombia we trip over goats and we kill people in the street! Do you know how offensive that is? Like we're Peruvians!*

Jay: *I don't get how one dog keeps you awake when you grew up sleeping through cockfights and revolutions.*

Manny: *In Colombia, they open presents at midnight and stay up 'til morning.*
Jay: *I'm sure they do, but if you notice from the absence of goats in the streets, we're not in Colombia.*

Before picketing ABC, writing your congressman and boycotting *Modern Family*, keep in mind that Gloria and Manny share a happy, loving life with Jay and their newfound family. They definitely give as well as get. As you watch the show, you rarely feel sorry for the Latino duo—quite the opposite. Typically, you feel sorry for whoever is on the other end of their sharp-shooting tongues:

> **Gloria:** *In my culture, men take great pride in doing physical labor.*
> **Jay:** *I know. That's why I hire people from your culture.*
> **Gloria:** *(laughs) You're too funny. I'm going to share that one with my next husband when we're spending all your money.*

> **Gloria:** *You're his family now and that means only one thing: you be the wind in his back, not the spit in his face.*
> **Jay:** *What?*
> **Gloria:** *Something my mom always says. It's gorgeous in Spanish.*

> **Jay:** *I'm not here to spit in your face; I'm here to blow at your back.*
> **Everybody:** *What?*
> **Jay:** *It's supposed to sound better in Spanish.*
> **Gloria:** *Voy a ser la brisa en tu espalda, no quien te escupa en la frente.*
> **Everybody:** *Oh!*
> **Cam:** *That's beautiful.*

> **Jay:** *[on teaching Manny chess] I'm going to teach him the real version, not the Colombian version. We actually use the pieces to play the game, not smuggle stuff out of the country.*
> **Gloria:** *I know what Colombian piece you won't be playing with.*

The comebacks aren't all just verbal jousting. Sometimes Gloria gets tired of the constant jokes at her expense and she retaliates, such as the time Gloria is upset about her grandmother appearing in her dreams. Gloria believes that her grandmother is chastising her for abandoning her Colombian customs. The solution is to make a traditional Colombian dinner, whereupon Jay quips that his dead uncle appeared in his dream and wants a steak. Gloria becomes very angry and demands Jay make amends by following the Colombian customs of slapping a chicken to keep death off the food and wearing shoes around his neck to symbolize walking in the footsteps of her ancestors. Jay obliges, because, as Cam puts it, "*She scares me when she yells in Spanish*." While Jay exuberantly slaps a chicken, Gloria explains to the camera:

> **Gloria:** *I made all that up. That's not a real custom in Colombia. We're not lunatics! But if you mess with us, we mess with you. THAT'S the custom.*

In this case, Gloria's grandmother does have a point, however. Manny is losing his cultural sense. And his grasp of the Spanish language.

> **Gloria:** *You're starting to forget your Spanish. You don't practice.*
> **Manny:** *Lo siento, mama. Estoy embarazada.*
> **Gloria:** *You just told me you're pregnant.*
> **Jay:** *Congratulations. You're glowing.*

Cam and Mitchell's relationship is the one most loaded with cultural clashes. Everyone talks about it, tweets it, debates it, blogs it and the opinions are as varied as Cam's wardrobe. With the way society views it, it's a wonder they're able to maintain a relationship, let alone thrive and bring up their daughter. Yes, I'm talking about Cam being from a farm in Missouri and Mitchell being a dazzling urbanite lawyer.

Cam: *Mitchell is a snob.*
Mitchell: *No, n-no, I'm discerning.*
Cam: *Official slogan for snobs. When we first met he would't even look at me because I was a hick from the farm in Missouri and he's a big city mouse.*
Mitchell: *Who says city mouse?*
Cam: *Country mice.*

While the audience enjoys watching the conflict, it leaves many wondering how they manage to stay together. Maybe it's because of their shared interests – like visiting the lavender ranch in Hawaii. Oh, wait. No, Mitchell went by himself and Cam stayed behind at the pool with Lily. Well, maybe they don't share many interests, but they do try. Like when Mitchell plans an incredibly over the moon—actually over the rainbow—blow your mind party for Cam's fortieth birthday. However, since he was born on February 29, Cam feels it's his tenth birthday, and the theme is the Wizard of Oz, complete with yellow brick road, a scarecrow and a girl in pigtails with a cute puppy in a picnic basket. Just as the festivities are getting set up, Mitchell has a revelation:

Mitchell: *How could I miss the connection? A month after the most devastating twister to hit Cam's home town, I throw a party based on gay cinema's most famous tornado.*

The performers, decorations, food, all of it are bundled away faster than a Kansas house in a twister and Mitchell is left without a fall back plan. He manages to book a motor yacht, but too many passengers and a dead seal nix that plan:

Luke: *It smells like puke married poop and had the ceremony in my nose.*
Manny: *You paint with words.*

The family winds up at an amusement park, because Mitchell finally has the right epiphany:

Mitchell: *All this time I've been trying to figure out what Cam wanted for his birthday, and he'd been telling me all along. He wanted to be ten.*

While Cam is the more open and thoughtful one in the relationship, his farm roots affect his city style more than he cares to admit. For instance, he and Mitchell visit the homestead in Missouri and it's revealed that Cam hasn't told his grandmother (Grams) about his relationship. Instead, he introduces Mitchell as the new farmhand, Bud. While trapped in a shelter waiting out a tornado warning, Cam opens up to Grams. Her response was not as heartwarming as expected. It turns out that Missouri may be the "Show Me" state, but not the "Show Me Everything" state...

Cam *(on revealing his engagement to Grams)*: *After the initial shock, Grams softened a bit. She even agreed to attend the wedding.*
Mitchell: *Standing outside with a sign.*

Not only is Cam a farm boy to Mitchell's city boy, Cam's a dreamer to Mitchell's realism or, as Cam, sees it, a Pritchett. This comes to a head when Cam tells his story about Punkin Chunkin. Cam recounts how he and some friends managed to slingshot a pumpkin down a football field. Cam, Phil, Gloria, and Manny help set up the pumpkin and it only makes it about 15 yards. Jay, Mitchell and Claire give them a hard time, but then pitch in and the pumpkin sails down the field and smashes into Claire's minivan. While Mitchell will never be the dreamer, artist and farm boy that Cam is, overcoming challenges like how best to chunk a punkin down a field helps him get a little closer to the man of his dreams. Cam continues to soar:

> **Cam:** *There are dreamers, and there are realists in this world. You would think the dreamers would find the dreamers and the realists find the realists, but more often than not, the opposite is true. You see, the dreamers need the realists to keep them from soaring too close to the sun. And well, without the dreamers, they might never get off the ground.*

Joined in by the rest of the dreamers...

> **Luke:** *Why are there giant lollipops all over our front yard, and why do they taste so bad?*
> **Alex:** *Because they're made of cardboard, mouthbreather.*
> **Phil:** *Hey! The world needs dreamers, Luke. Never stop licking things.*

There is one aspect of Cam and Mitchell's relationship that they share equally. It's one of the most important facets of their lives together and the one they're most clueless about. Not just because there's a foreign culture involved, but, like most parents with a newborn, at times they have no idea what to do with a tiny person who depends on them for everything. It's time to discuss their adopted Vietnamese daughter, Lily.

Like all new parents, Cam and Mitchell feel pressure to be perfect and to give their little girl a dream life, but they struggle with knowing how to take care of a little girl—especially one from a foreign culture. Of course, when you're clueless, turn to a professional. Who should know more about raising an Asian child than a female, Asian pediatrician? Enter Dr. Miura. Cam becomes friendly with the young woman in an attempt to bring an Asian influence into Lily's life. Of course, it's quickly overdone:

> **Mitchell:** *Take it down a notch, we're trying to make a*

friend, not initiate a three-way.

Cam continues to impress upon Dr. Miura that they're raising Lily ever mindful to her Vietnamese culture:

Cam: *We're planning on taking her to a restaurant for some pho. Is that how it's pronounced? Pho [Fuh]?*
Dr. Miura: *I have no idea. I'm from Denver.*

Cameron: *This is a special soup called 'pho' [fuh].*
Lily: *You told me not to say that word.*

She does assure them they are fine parents and Lily will survive their missteps, but it's not enough. Along with Gloria, they take Lily to a Vietnamese restaurant to ensure she learns about her heritage. As a side effect, Cam and Mitchell want to convince her she's not gay, just because her Daddies are. In the course of the dinner, the three adults manage to imply insults towards every ethnic, cultural and racial faction represented in the restaurant:

Lily *[to the Vietnamese Waitress]*: *I HATE Vietnam!*

Mitchell: *Honey, you're not gay. You're just confused. Oh my God! What is wrong with me?*

Luckily, Gloria is there to help, just as Cam and Mitchell are about to give up. Her rant is not triggered by what's transpiring in the restaurant, but is really a response to her earlier fears that Manny's losing his cultural identity:

Gloria: *That's the problem with this country! Nobody cares about where they come from anymore! They just want cheeseburgers and prep school and forget they come from Colombia!*

Gloria: *I'm just afraid they're going to grow up and become* *boring old white people.*

Timing is everything and two elderly white people walk by just as she delivers this last comment. Now it's Cam's turn to apologize and make everything better:

Cam: *Uh, most of our friends are white. [two black people go by] OK, can everybody just calm down and go back to their own conversations?*

It's obvious that the underlying issues are that each, in their own way, are feeling different. This revelation leads to an almost preachy lesson from the guys that a family is a group of people who love each other and not just because they came from the same place:

Cam: *[to Lily] You know, you just caused a scene in a restaurant, and you can't get any more like your daddies than that.*

Gloria feels better and contemplates taking Manny and Joe to Colombia for the summer. Mitchell assures her that this is a great idea and adds that all should get more in touch with their roots, their culture, and Cam agrees. After all, who wouldn't?

Cam: *Absolutely! I think we'd all be better off if people would go back to where they came from!*
Mitchel: *(awkward) I'll...go pull the car around.*

6 Do This, Don't Do That

"Signs," Five Man Electrical Band, 1971

Along with the laughs, Modern Family brings numerous social issues to the small screen. What gives them power is not just the standard formula of making us laugh at our foibles. Instead, the writers bring out how human beings would really react when faced with situations that make them uncomfortable, unhappy or even threaten their way of life. Sometimes the reactions do make the audience laugh. It is a sitcom, after all, but at other times they bring on frustration, tears and, occasionally, a cringe or two. One of the most controversial social issues in the program is Cam and Mitchell's gay relationship. There are many outliers from this, but just the basic fact that they're together is a core conflict, one that even they struggle with, such as when they're preparing to take Lily to day care:

> **Mitchell:** *We're gonna be judged enough as the only gay parents there; I don't wanna be the late ones too. Wow, paisley and pink. Was there something wrong with the fishnet tank top.*
>
> **Cam:** *Obviously not; I'm wearing it underneath. Kidding. Just chill, please.*
>
> **Mitchell:** *I'm sorry; I just wanna make a good first*

impression.

Cam: *You mean you wanna fit in and not terrify the villagers?*

Mitchell: *No- hey, come on. Today is about Lily, alright? Her future best friend might be in that class and I don't wanna... rub anyone the wrong way. Can you please just... change your shirt.*

Cam: *Fine. You know what, I'll just go put on a pair of khakhis, maybe a polo shirt and everybody'll think we're a couple of straight golfing buddies who just decided to have a kid together.*

They do work it out; especially when they realize not being themselves is making them crazy, and when another gay couple arrives at the day care and everyone fawns over them. Unfortunately, this exemplifies that their revelations come, not from a place of strength within, but from the observation that society accepts—and loves—others similar to them:

Cam: *Look at those queens. I would've killed with this crowd, but you had to clip my wings, which you used to be the wind beneath.*

Mitchell: *I know, I'm so- This class has turned me into a complete monster. I'm ju- I'll make it up to you. Let's just go.*

Teacher: *Okay, it's time for Parents' Dance! Everybody dance for your baby!*

Mitchell: *You wanna do it, don't you?*

Cam: *I do. I wanna dance for my baby.*

Mitchell: *Alright, go on. Get in there.*

Cam: *Sure?*

Mitchell: *Make that horsey move. Go ahead.*

Cam: *[runs off; does horsey move in the circle; runs out] Oh, I think I hurt myself.*

Additionally, various scenarios show the couple's

discomfort with their gayness. While at home they celebrate their relationship, outside it's as if they're teenagers who have just come out. Halloween is the premiere gay holiday and Mitchell celebrates it by arriving at his office in his Spiderman suit, and only a *douche and a tool* are dressed up. He spends the rest of the episode trying to get back into normal clothes without his straight co-workers discovering he's in costume. When Mitchell is ultimately outed, instead of greeting the fanfare with panache, he cowers in his car and tries to ignore the overtures from the other two who're dressed up. This denouement is a social miss, as it's difficult to tell what point is being made other than that it's fun to laugh at people who are different.

While Cam and Mitchell struggle with external perception, the people delivering the external view struggle as well. Claire, as Mitchell's sister, is tolerant of their relationship, but acceptance cracks at times. The aforementioned Halloween meltdown is one example. In that instance, it's not that she's against their relationship, but rather at how it impacts her traditions and enjoyment of holidays and family life. In Jay's case, he wants his son to be happy, but wishes that Mitchell was 'normal,' and he's not the only parent that feels that way.

On several occasions, Jay interacts with Cam's father, Merle Tucker. They bond over discomfort with their sons' choices and disconnect for similar reasons, particularly when it comes to who's the female. Both fathers feel that if their son is the 'man' in the relationship, it makes it easier to believe that their progeny is normal. While Merle claims to be comfortable with his son's choice in life partners, he cracks when put to the test:

> **Merle** *[talking to Jay in the steam room at the country club]: I'd like to think I've evolved on the subject. We got a couple of lesbo swans in the pond. They seem pretty*

happy.
Jay: [*Sighs*]

Howard: [*entering the steam room*] *Hey, Jay.*
Jay: *Hey, Howard, Larry. This is my, uh... This is my friend Merle and he's visiting from Missouri.*
Howard: *Ooh, the "show me" state.*
Jay: *Don't say that in here!*
[*Everyone laughs*]
Howard: *So, what brings you to town, Merle?*
Merle: *Well, uh, my... our... Jay's and my... kids are getting married today.*
Howard: *Congratulations. Isn't that nice? Father of the bride, father of the groom taking a steam together the day of the wedding.*
Merle: *Yeah, something like that.*
Howard: *The day my son got married... piece of cake. But the day I lost my little girl... Ohh, that wrecked me. So, which one of you has to suffer through that today?*
Merle: *You know what? It's too hot in here.*
Jay: *Yeah. Let's go. ... Mm-hmm. Real evolved. Your swans would be ashamed.*

This conversation took place during the episodes that specifically focused on another hot social topic – gay marriage. When Cam and Mitchell finally decide—and are finally allowed—to tie the knot, the happy day is spread across two episodes. There are rampant references to gay mannerisms sprinkled throughout, some bordering on pure stereotypes, but the references are tempered with introspections that take the sting out of them. One of the funnier subplots stems from the not-so-funny blowup between Jay and Mitchell. The latter comes about when Jay reveals his true feelings about Cam and Mitchell's upcoming nuptials and Mitchell fires back. Specifically, Mitchell asks why Jay hasn't invited any of his friends from the country club:

Jay: *I don't think I'm out of line suggesting my friends don't want to see a father/son dance at a gay wedding.*
Mitchell: *There is no father/son dance, Dad.*

Jay: *When did I quit having the opportunity to be me? Why can't I ever say when I'm uncomfortable about something? I didn't choose to be uncomfortable. I was born this way.*
Mitchell: *If it really makes you that uncomfortable, then don't come to the wedding.*

Nothing particularly funny about that interchange, nor by the follow-on during the wildfire scare when Jay implies it's going against God's will for two men to marry:

Jay: *The fire was an act of God, not that God sent a fireball down to keep you guys from getting married.*

Cam: *"We're experiencing signs of the Apocalypse."*
1. The sky turned dark *[Mitchell: Because of the fire]*
2. Flood *[pregnant Sal's water broke]*
3. A swarm of Lucases *[the angry family whose wedding venue they crashed]*
4. Famine *[Pepper: Just get another caterer here or these people will be eating butterfly bisque!]*
5. The Four Hoarse Men *[Pepper, Steven, Stefan and Longinus all lost their voices]*

Just as the boys are about to admit defeat and cancel their wedding, Jay steps in and agrees that this isn't the way they should do it. As Mitchell rants, "We *get* it, *it's against God's will, we should not be doing this,*" Jay cuts him off and explains they should move the event to his county club. "*That place needs shaking up.*" The ending scene is a beautiful wedding with all the people they love taking part. The takeaway from the wedding plotline is that while families may want the best for their loved ones, they don't always know how to express themselves or show support. And, just because they support decisions that may lead to alternate lifestyles, that doesn't mean they're comfortable with all the implications of those lifestyles. This is all a part of life and human nature, like having children and being a real family, something Cam and Mitchell want badly – badly enough to travel to Vietnam to accomplish. Since the two aren't perceived as being terribly responsible, nobody expects them to want a child:

> **Mitch:** *We didn't go to Vietnam for pleasure we kinda got some big news.*
> **Jay:** *Oh God, if Cam comes out here with boobs I'm leaving.*

In particular, it's clear that Jay isn't comfortable with them adopting a child and believes that Cam is usually too dramatic; too over the top. He isn't proved wrong when Cam presents Lily in a *Lion King* like gesture, complete with music and lights and a flowing robe. Eventually, Jay warms to the idea out of love for his son and expresses himself in a typical Jay fashion by managing to insult an entire way of life, while attempting to accept another:

> **Jay:** *What do I know? It's not like I wrote the book on fatherhood. Been trying all my life to get it right, and I'm still screwing up. Right, Manny?*
> **Manny:** *I wrote a song about it in the car.*
> **Jay:** *[about Lily] Let's see the little potsticker!*

Once Lily is settled into their world, the two daddies struggle with the same types of doubts and insecurities that any new parents experience. *Are they good enough? Will Lily grow up to be successful? Will she be well adjusted and happy?* This intensifies because of their gay relationship and they not only second-guess many choices, but over react in hilarious ways, such as when they're on the plane getting ready to fly to Hawaii:

> **Passenger 3:** *Look at that baby with those cream puffs.*
> **Mitchell:** *Oh. Excuse me. Excuse me. This baby would've grown up in a crowded orphanage if it hadn't been for us "cream puffs". And you know what? Note to all of you who judge-*
> **Cam:** *Mitchell!*
> **Mitchell:** *Hear this! Love knows no race, creed—*
> **Cam:** *Mitchell!*
> **Mitchell:** *or gender. And shame on you, you small-minded, ignorant few who—*
> **Cam:** *Mitchell! Mitchell!*
> **Mitchell:** *What?*
> **Cam:** *She's got the cream puffs*
> *[Mitchell takes his seat and Cam stands up.]*
> **Cam:** *We'd like to pay for everyone's head phones.*

When Lily is a typical child—she bites, she drops the F-bomb at a wedding, she gets into makeup, smearing all over her face—the two men blame themselves for not being better parents. Especially when she becomes 'snarky' such as saying *"Should I call you a Waam-bulance?"* and *"C'mon ladies [to her dads], today."* Mitchell is convinced she's picking this up at home and he and Cam try to modify their behavior, even when it costs them invitations to the blow-out gay party of the year because they won't act catty about a friend's home perm. *"Be honest—doesn't he look like a chia pet?"* Since Lily is standing beside them, the guys won't rise to the bait and are thus 'uninvited.' This is all for nothing, they find out later, because it's Claire's behavior Lily is imitating, not theirs. In a similar situation, Lily's first word is *Mommy*, not because she misses a female influence in her life, but because her favorite doll says *"Mommy."*

Yes, being new parents is tough and stressful, but lighten up, guys! She's turning out just fine. Okay, the biting needs to stop, but some children are just biters. Additionally, they should keep an eye on the little girl and stop misplacing her:

> **Mitchell**: *[They've lost Lily in a banana plantation] Why did you dress her in jungle prints?*
> **Cam:** *I thought it would be cute!*
> **Mitchell**: *She's gonna think she's back in Vietnam!*

Any time a child enters a relationship it can cause strain, and Cam and Mitchell are no different, especially when Cam finds out his name is not on the adoption papers. It reveals the insecurity Mitchell experienced when the time came to set up the paperwork. Convinced that Cam was going to run out on them, Mitchell left his name off the papers to avoid a legal snarl in the future. Was this because they're gay? Not in any sense. It's the natural panic two human beings experience when faced with a life-altering decision. In the real world, it's sad and can cause pain and even bring about what it was meant to alleviate— a break up. On *Modern Family*, it's another reason to talk something out, laugh a little, and come together with a hug at the end. And file new paperwork. And even joke about their little ward:

> **Mitchell:** *Quick, turn off your car.*
> **Haley:** *Why? It's in park, I think.*
> **Mitchell:** *I have a judgy, green neighbor. He had the nerve to come over here and tell me I'm not green enough.*
> **Haley:** *Shut up! You're super green!*
> **Mitchell:** *Thank you! I'm recycling a dollhouse. [Whispering about Lily] I even recycled a child.*

Okay, they're a family. Now, somebody has to take care of the mundane details such as paying the mortgage and buying food, and who pays for the Godzilla-sized packages of diapers for Lily. Cam introduces Mitchell to Costco and suddenly they have to buy a shed to stockpile supplies. Mitchell's career hovers in the background with typical issues and concerns. *Will he fit in? Should he go for the money and defend big Corporations or should he go for less money and fight for societal issues such as the environment or gay rights? Should he wear his Spiderman costume to the office for Halloween or stick to the three-piece suit?* Decisions, decisions, decisions. To focus on important social issues such as the ecology and the importance of being green, Mitchell does take a job as an environmental lawyer and uses the opportunity to share his passion with his next-door neighbor:

> **Mitchell:** *I'm an environmental lawyer, so you know, I'm pretty green.*
> **Asher:** *So's your lawn. I went drought-tolerant -- succulents, indigenous plants, rock garden.*
> **Lily:** *My other daddy says your yard looks like a litter box.*
> **Asher:** *She's a cute kid. I remember when she was in disposable diapers.*

While the series does a wink and a nod to Mitchell's career struggles, Cam comes front and center. Depressed when Lily goes to kindergarten, he takes a job as a music teacher at the high school, where his students and faculty alike love him. Combine that with Cam's extracurricular pursuit as a football coach, and the Pritchett-Tucker family is not just making it, but thriving. In addition, Lily doesn't even have to work in a rice paddy or a sweat shop. Sweet.

Now that they're tucked away, what about the Dunphy's?

Since the Dunphy's are the *typical* middle-class American family, Phil is the breadwinner. He's a relatively successful realtor and Claire is the stay-at-home mom. All is well, for the most part. That is, until Phil hits a dry spell and the family gets concerned. Luckily, it's a *Modern Family*, and everyone wants to pitch in and help. Like Luke:

> **Luke:** *[holding a music keyboard]* *Hey dad, I think I found a place online where I can sell this organ. Can you drive me to the black market?*
> **Phil:** *I think they mean a different kind of organ, buddy.*

Hey, at least he's trying. In a good way. Phil does try to get back on top by playing dirty with a barracuda of a realtor, but fails miserably. Again, Luke comes to the rescue, and this time he scores:

> **Phil:** *[a rival realtor has stolen his account]* *You're not gonna believe this. Mitzi got the listing.*
> **Claire:** *Oh, no, honey. That's awful!*
> **Phil:** *She cheated, she lied, and she won. Kids, gather round.*
> **Haley:** *Again, we are gathered.*
> **Phil:** *You want to get ahead? Don't play by the rules. Turns out nice guys finish last in this cold dog-eat-dog world.*
> **Luke:** *It's not fair. Why don't you play dirty, too? You could take her down.*
> **Claire:** *Oh, honey, 'cause your dad is a better man than that. He has values and morals and...*
> **Phil:** *Shh... You, keep talking.*
> **Luke:** *Well, just off the top of my head, you could take my spy pen an record her admitting what she did. And then you could play it for those people so they'd realize what a jerk she is.*
> **Claire:** *Your dad is never gonna do that.*
> **Phil:** *You're a regular chatterbox today. Get me that pen!*

This plan fails miserably because—well—because Phil is Phil. Enter Luke. Again. In a grocery store, he runs into the evil realtor, Mitzi, and asks her why she's so mean to his dad, especially when he's so preoccupied with Haley's college payments and something about a balloon payment coming up on the house. The realtor caves and gives a listing to Phil, but it turns out it was all set up by Phil and Luke to play on her humanity. It's weird, but Phil is back to being the successful breadwinner. This works for Claire, until the kids all go to school and she's left with empty nest syndrome. She's beautiful, smart, educated and has a winning personality.

Whoa...Stop right there. Remember the unlikable part? Claire's existence is rife with unsuccessful social interactions. Either she can't get along—such as when she takes a job with Phil's arch rival, Gil Thorpe—or others don't care for her—like when she runs for town council. So what's a resume-challenged, closing in on middle-age, stay-at-home mom supposed to do? Particularly when her very successful friend shows up with the riches that Claire gave up to have a somewhat insane family. Yes, there's only one real solution, which is to give in and take the job Dad's been dangling in front of her for years. Claire goes to work for Jay at his closet business, and it's ironic that Jay has a closet business given his son is.... Anyway, I digress.

Claire takes a job at Jay's business and works frantically to make a name for herself and not rely solely on being the boss's daughter. She makes headway until she manages to knock down a whole warehouse full of closet displays, just like setting a series of dominoes into motion. She's thankful for being the boss's daughter then and experiencing the privilege of being forgiven for such a heinous act. Jay is forgiving—even tolerant—and then lowers the boom. Claire has to spend the weekend cleaning up the mess in the warehouse. Yes, membership does have its privileges.

This presents the other woman in Jay's life—Gloria. She has a closet the size of most people's bedrooms, a wardrobe to die for, and a life of luxury. Yet, she drags

Cam and Phil and anyone else who will brave the 'hood back to her old neighborhood and the beauty shop she loved to work in. Gloria is skilled and resourceful as well as beautiful. (More about this later.) As a sneak preview, she's not just a gold-digging pretty face and pretty boobs. (But more later.) Then it gets interesting. For now, the discussion is about Gloria and Jay's May / December romance and what it brings out in others—like exes.

Jay's ex-wife, DeDe, is the one that asked for a divorce. However, when her life isn't as exciting or glamorous or even as happy as she anticipated, she arrives back on the scene and blames everything on Gloria. She disrupts their wedding by getting Drunk and Disorderly, with a capital 'D.' At first, DeDe appears well-behaved and accepting of the union to be, but quickly deteriorates into a jealous mess:

> **DeDe:** *[At Jay and Gloria's wedding] When I first met Gloria and Jay told me they were getting married; I thought it was a match made in heaven; Jay's money and Gloria's boobs.*

When DeDe is dragged out of the reception screaming and kicking and her butt covered in birthday cake, this situation became known as *The Incident.* Ah yes, love. It brings out the best in people.

Expectations also bring out the best in people. The entire family expects Alex to be successful at anything she attempts, except for being social and popular:

> **Claire:** *How did you get so smart?*
> **Alex:** *I've always assumed adoption or baby switch.*

> **Alex:** *Dumb guys go for dumb girls and smart guys go for dumb girls. What do smart girls get?*
> **Phil:** *Cats, mostly.*

Regardless of how it came about, Alex believes that the family's hope for success lies squarely on her shoulders. This is a huge amount of pressure on a teenager:

> **Alex:** *It's junior year, I have to get good grades. Don't you know how competitive it is out there? Stop pressuring me!*
> **Haley:** *You know, this is what happens to kids when they're not sexually active.*

The pressure is so bad that Alex wants to see a therapist. In this family, who's the best one to choose an appropriate doctor? Alex, of course:

> **Alex:** *I wanna see a therapist. I did some research. Dr. Gregory Clark -- highly recommended, specializes in teenagers and is covered by our insurance. I booked a double session with him today, and since you guys have the open house, I will be taking the bus.*
> **Claire:** *...OK.*
> **Phil:** *That sounds good. [Whispering to Claire] She's like a self-cleaning oven.*

The pressure, the lack of friends, the teasing from her family—in spite of these things, Alex does manage to have some fun, like when Cam serves Luke *facon* (fake bacon made from soy) without realizing Luke is severely allergic to soy. Since Cam is watching the children while the parents and Mitchell are bailing Haley out of jail for underage drinking, he herds everyone up and takes them to the hospital with Luke. While the doctors are treating Luke for his allergic reaction, Alex joins a group of interns and makes rounds. She wows everyone with her knowledge and expertise right up until she faints from the sight of blood during a Caesarian birth.

Huh.

Looks as if Alex isn't as perfect as the family thought she was.

Kind of sad.

This leads us to Haley. No one expects much of her except to be cute and popular and maybe get into Community College. Which she does, but then gets kicked out for assaulting an officer when she was arrested for drinking at a party. Also kind of sad. Throughout the series, Haley is portrayed as a drinker and a partier, but without suffering any consequences. It's no surprise when she can't cut it at college, but even then there are no real consequences. Phil and Claire attempt to intervene by confronting her about her future at a restaurant. This time, Haley doesn't drink, but her parents do, and they try to set her up with the busboy:

> **Haley:** *Look, I have no problem drinking. I can literally do it standing on my head. But A ,not with my parents. Plus also I needed to stay sharp because they were obviously up to something and I was in no mood. I barely got 10 hours of sleep last night.*

> **Phil:** *He seems like a real go-getter huh?*
> **Haley:** *Why, cause he goes and gets things?*

Maybe it isn't that difficult to figure out why Haley has a drinking problem. At least somebody was able to drive home.

Woven through this storyline is the lesson that children misbehaving can be tied to their parents and what they learn at home. This same theme integrates into other story lines as well. Mitchell and Claire always have to be right and refuse to share their belongings. Lily mirrors this behavior:

> **Lily:** *[pushing Luke away from Cameron] My daddy!*
> **Mitchell:** *Lily, no! I'm sorry, Luke.*

Luke: *[glaring at Lily] This isn't over.*

Cam: *Oh, my God, Mitchell. She's getting worse. I have turned her into a pushy little entitled monster on her way to a rap sheet and a bracelet on her ankle.*
[Cam glances at Lily and whimpers]
Cam: *Oh, she has a bracelet on her ankle.*

Claire: *None of you believe me so I got proof. You should all be sucking it right now!*
Gloria: *Claire, please, enough with the sucking it! They're children!*

As it turns out, Lily's inability to share comes from Mitchell, not Cam. Claire is, of course, just Claire. This tendency is what led her to spend six hours tracking down a security tape to prove she was in the right. What do Mitchell and Claire have in common? Jay. What does Jay have to be? Right.

Riiiight…. Mystery solved.

Of course, children don't always take after their parents. Sometimes they rebel and go against their parents' wishes and hopes, and parents have to understand, even if they don't like it. It's called *growing up*. Luke doesn't want to learn magic, Claire doesn't want to work for Jay in the closet business, and Manny wants a girlfriend in spite of Gloria wanting him to remain a little boy forever:

Claire *[trying to convince Phil that Luke can quit magic if he wants to]***:** *Let's play this out. Even if he is one in a million, what's our best case scenario? He becomes what?*
Phil *[excitedly]* **and Claire** *[reluctantly]***:** *A professional magician!*

7 Fantasy

Earth Wind and Fire, 1977

Modern Family has interesting story lines, clever writing and believable characters. It's fun to tune in and find out what everyone's up to and laugh and cry and cringe along with them. Think about how the series could be made better. Let's face it, the only thing more fun than a great sitcom is the opportunity to be an armchair admiral; to participate in a rousing game of *What if*???

The story line with the biggest target on its forehead is Cam and Mitchell's. Previously there was a discussion on how this is a family-oriented sitcom. Long, passionate, steamy love scenes don't really have a place on the couch alongside Lily and Manny and Luke.

However.

Mitchell and Cam could be more amorous. A much-discussed scene in the first season showed Claire and Phil kissing, while Cam and Mitchell hugged—platonically—in the background. In addition, the two men are constantly snarking at each other, without exhibiting a lot of affection for each other. This is revealed in an episode where they believe Lily is picking up their sarcastic behavior. *"Cry me a river. Today, ladies! [to her fathers]"* and, of course, the most popular *"Should I call you a wambulance?"* This inspires the

Pritchett-Tucker couple to change not because they want to be better partners and soul mates to each other, but for their adopted daughter. This is admirable to an extent, but it would be refreshing if they focused as much on each other and they do on everyone else, as opposed to Valentine's Day where they spent the whole time trying to determine who Mitchell's assistant, Broderick, has a crush on. Hopefully, now that they're married [spoiler alert!], they'll treat each other with more affection and respect and, since they've already been seen in the same bed together (no *Bewitched* or *The Dick Van Dyke Show* beds for this modern couple), the upcoming seasons may even show them getting hot and heavy. Once Lily has gone to bed.

The fantasy ride continues with the other Pritchett child, Claire. As a stay-at-home mom, she has some challenging roles, but it's easy to believe that an intelligent, confident, really, really tightly wound woman such as Claire would get bored staying at home once the children are in school. She does expand her horizons by running for the local council, flipping a house with Cam and even taking a job with Phil's archrival, Gil Thorpe. As alluded to in songs, poems and even movies (*Mars Attacks!* Comes to mind...), two out of three ain't bad. Wait. In this case, one out of three ain't bad. Well...maybe it is bad. So bad that, eventually, Claire agrees to work with Jay in the family closet business and she does well, in spite of the stigma of being the boss's daughter. At least in this case, the company's employees don't like her because of the nepotism and not for her personally. Baby steps. Baby steps...

To round out the Pritchett clan, enter Jay. Of all the characters, Jay is the most stereotypical and has the possibility of losing the ability to deliver the laughs. His primary redeeming features are that he's rich and generous, hidden in a crusty, 'take no prisoners' / 'tell it like it is', bullet-proof shell. So what if he lost his business? Or sold out and retired? Would he finally focus solely on his lovely wife? Or would he age twenty years and sink into a gray haze of waiting for the grim reaper? Or, the obvious question, would Gloria grab Manny and run? An interesting twist would be if Jay focused on little Fulgencio and became a stay-at-home dad while Gloria took up the bread-winning role in four-inch heels.

Gloria is not all gorgeousness and sex appeal. She's had plenty of successful businesses as well. Throughout the series, she has told stories of driving a cab, winning beauty pageants, working at a hair salon, and even escaping from the horrid little Colombian village in which she spent her childhood. The latter was by striding across her sister's back in stiletto heels, but it was still a success. Just imagine what she could do in a closet. Business. Closet business. Especially if shoes were involved:

> **Gloria:** *Let me tell you a story. There was this girl who entered a beauty contest. She was nervous because she was very scared that she was going to lose.*
>
> **Claire:** *Let me guess. You won.*
>
> **Gloria:** *Of course I did. I was talking about my cousin Maria Conchita. She had a nose like a toucan and had to stuff her big body into this little bikini. She came in dead last.*
>
> **Claire:** *Why are you telling me all this?*
>
> **Gloria:** *The point is, she faced her fear and it didn't kill her. What killed her was the bus that hit her two weeks later.*

With that kind of attitude, how can she fail?

The adults in *Modern Family* are typically strong, practical and devoted to creating a good life for their children. Phil is no exception. He works hard as a realtor, even in the face of difficult competition from his competitors such as Gil Thorpe and Mitzi Roth. Phil provides well for his family, but in addition to being a shrewd negotiator and businessman, he is also a dreamer and an inventor. Luke typically helps him with his plans and it's fun to watch the two of them scheming together. Sometimes it works, such as the time they put popcorn into pancake batter to Flip Jacks—self-popping pancakes. Sometimes it doesn't work, like the "Real Headscratcher®", which nearly takes out a chunk of scalp:

Phil: *Hey friend. You look like you had a rough day at the office.*

Luke: *The stress from my job at the Robot Assassin Factory is too much to take. Aw, shoot me an aspirin, pal.*

Phil: *Maybe someday. But until then, try this on for size. The real HeadScratcher features 32 patent pending nogginizers that gently massage your scalp. In a soothing purr of motorized delight.*

Luke: *Wow. It feels great, and it looks good too. It's a real life saver.*

Phil: *You mean, a real Head Scratcher?*

Phil / Luke: *Hahahahahahhaha.*

Phil: *TM.*

After visiting with a nerdy friend from high school who became a millionaire by following the adage *"What would Phil do?"* Phil realizes that what's holding him back is Claire. She shot down all his best ideas such as:

The Rice Pudding Franchise – *Works for all chewing abilities*

Adult Tricycles – *Just try to fall off*

The Aspirin Gun – *Some people have a hard time swallowing*

Since this is the fantasy tour, what if Phil managed to sell one of his ideas on *Shark Tank?* Or devised an invention to augment Jay's closet business and became a partner with his father-in-law in spite of Claire. Now THAT would be a fun episode to watch. Claire's astonished face—the one where her cheek muscle twitches—would be great to watch while she tries to comprehend that her husband is not a complete goofball. Partial goofball, maybe, but not a complete one.

Now that the adults are covered, what about the children? Taking them in different directions from their typical paths wouldn't be that much of a stretch. The first one that comes to mind is a classic switcheroo. Alex could fall for a handsome dumb guy, while Haley could lose her heart to a nerdy Einstein. Phil, an idiot savant where his children are concerned, recognizes the danger of Haley continuing on her current path:

> **Phil:** *Hayley, you're not going to quit that job!*
> **Haley:** *What? Where is this coming from?*
> **Phil:** *Your future, and it's not pretty.*
> **Haley:** *I don't get it. In the future, I'm not pretty?*
> **Phil:** *No, you hold up okay, but you end up divorcing five guys with nicotine fingers.*

The oldest Dunphy sibling has come close to breaking her stereotypical mold and this bleak vision of her future, but is yanked back from the precipice just as she's about to tumble:

> **Haley:** *Hey, check out that cute guy.*
> **Alex:** *He's out of your league. He's reading a book.*
> **Haley:** *Yeah, I know.*

Haley even made out with her brainy tutor. Returning to the house too quickly, Claire witnesses this and doesn't approve. Not because Haley is making out, but because Claire knows Haley is still going out with Dylan. Excited about ridding her daughter of what she perceives to be an albatross around her neck, Claire convinces Haley that she has to break up with Dylan. Haley agrees and breaks up with Dylan through a text message. She holds firm until she sees Dylan in a coffee shop, a girl's sweater on the seat beside him. Haley doesn't know it belongs to her father, who's comforting Dylan and wearing women's clothes. In a fit of jealous irrationality, Haley begs Dylan to come back and dumps the smart tutor, David. Dylan refuses, saying he *"needs time to date Dylan."* This makes both Haley and Phil sad, but also has the effect of leaving Haley without a boyfriend, smart or otherwise.

Boyfriends and relationships are always good for a laugh, but it would be interesting to see another change in Haley's storyline. At least once or twice a season, Haley is portrayed as drunk or hung-over or in the process of getting drunk. This has had small repercussions (condemnation from Claire) and huge implications (kicked out of college). Regardless of the magnitude of the misbehavior, she continues to escape punishment and have fun without consequences. An intriguing twist would be to have her face her irresponsibility. Of course, with Phil as her father—the cool dad who wants his children to have fun with him more than anything else—that would take a huge leap of imagination.

Then there's Alex. The smart kid who spends all her time practicing the cello or studying for tests or competing with brainiacs in spelling bees or other academic contests. The few boys she's dated are all nerdy mirrors of her. An exciting change would be to have her date the male equivalent of Haley. At least that would be better than the future painted for her in the episode *The Future Dunphys*. In that fantasy, the only serious relationship Alex has is with her cats.

Of the Dunphy children, the one the writers are expanding the most is Luke. In the wedding episode, it's revealed that Luke is depressed about having to follow Alex in high school. The teachers are always comparing him to his older, smarter sister and he feels he can't compare. He reveals this to Claire when they decide to take a jaunt in a canoe on the day of Cam and Mitchell's wedding. Unfortunately, they don't have oars. As Luke rails on about how smart Alex is and how she would figure out how to get back to shore, he uses the fishing rod to wrap a line around a tree and draw them in to shore. He doesn't recognize it was his idea and instead credits it to Alex. This is another time when Claire's twitchy astonished face is her only contribution to the situation. This would have been a great time for her to be a great mother and point out that Alex isn't the only one with good ideas. Way to go, Claire.

Manny is one of the more complex characters on the show—sophisticated, elegant, poet, football star, ladies' man. The writers are already experimenting with his persona, so he can be left alone for now. But what about Lily? She's cute, girlie, loves all things pink, snarky, biting sense of humor—the spitting image of her father, Cam. Since Cam has a rough and tumble side, why can't Lily? Just as Cam is an incredible football coach, it would be great to see Lily on a hockey team or trying out for Little League. She can still have pink bows in her hair, but she'd look adorable with dirt smudged on her cheek after sinking a puck or sliding into home.

8 Here in the Real World
Alan Jackson, 1990

The characters on *Modern Family* come together every week—several times a day on USA Network—and get into conflicts, have witty exchanges, learn something about themselves and life and acknowledge that they're a caring, loving family that are stronger when they're together, one half-hour slot at a time.   They're debated, quoted, criticized, laughed at / with, admired, and even loved. *Modern Family* presents an ideal that true modern families have a snowball's chance in hell of approaching.   They embody the allure of television—to escape the real world; to live someone else's life instead of your own.

But what happens behind the scenes? The characters are real people with real lives in the real world. What does their real world look like? Do they have insights from being on the show that mere watchers can't attain? Not really. In some cases, the typical viewer is probably glad they don't have their lives.

For instance, on October 3, 2013, Ariel Winter (Alex Dunphy) was removed from her home and placed under the temporary guardianship of her sister, Shanelle Workman. This happened after evidence was offered alleging the young woman had been emotionally abused by her mother, Crystal Workman. Accusations of physical abuse were found to be unsubstantiated. Crystal pointed out that the older sister, Shanelle, had barely been in Ariel's life. It wasn't until raises for the actors on *Modern Family* were announced that Shanelle showed any interest in her little sister. Regardless, Ariel remained in her sister's care as the mess was sorted out [1].

Unfortunately, almost a year later, the situation did not improve. In response to allegations of sexual abuse, Crystal claimed that Ariel had physically abused *her* by slapping her mother, screaming at her and then crying on cue when coached. The woman went on to say that the stress of dealing with her older daughter, Shanelle, had contributed to her contracting cancer [2]. Maybe this is why Alex's visits to her therapist on the program are so realistic.

Since Alex, the good girl of the series, is experiencing real world chaos, it would make sense that Haley, the wild child, would have an even more extreme lifestyle. However, that's not the case. She lives happily in Los Angeles with a protective boyfriend, Matt Propok, a maltipoo name Barkley and a loving, nurturing family. So loving that after a lifelong battle with kidney dysplasia, she underwent a kidney transplant with an organ donated from her father [3]. This is a far cry from the abuse and emotional distress survived by Ariel/Alex. In spite of this idealistic world, there are problems. Consider an incident that occurred in Australia this past February at a *Modern Family* event.

While attending a function hosted by Qantas Airlines, Sarah's breast was allegedly touched by an admiring fan. The police detained the man and Sarah left in obvious emotional distress. She later tweeted her friends and fans that she was sorry to have abandoned the party. Her boyfriend, Matt, was more outspoken in his tweets [4]:

Tweet 1: *To the a—hole who assaulted Sarah tonight I hope to God you don't see next week*

Tweet 2: *All Sarah wanted to do tonight was say hi to the girls who were waiting outside one douche can ruin it for everyone. Goodnight* [5].

Really? A man should not *"see next week"* because he tried to touch a celebrity? Now THAT'S extreme.

On an interesting note, the first tweet is no longer available although, as proven time and again, nothing is ever truly deleted on the Internet. Matt is wise to try to delete it.

Rounding out the Dunphy children is Luke, aka Nolan Gould. The lovable, klutzy, dumb kid that's Phil's Mini-Me. Claire's biggest fear for Luke is that he will grow up to be his father; confirmed when he's seen standing in a hardware store shaking his head in time with a paint can shaker. Phil, of course, is by his side, shaking his head even more vigorously. Early episodes had Luke getting his head stuck in the stair banisters. This character is so smooth and comfortable in his persona that an obvious assumption is that Nolan is similar in real life.

Not even close.

At thirteen, Nolan took the General Educational Development (GED) Test and tested out of high school after accelerating past 10 grades. He's a card-carrying member of Mensa and, in addition to acting, plays the double bass, banjo, didgeridoo, mandolin and sitar. He also wants to buy a theremin[6]. If you're a *Star Trek* fan, you know what the last one is. If you're not and you don't, don't be concerned, only geeks and nerds will look down on you for that lack of knowledge.

Talking about Luke/Nolan has to bring us to Phil or, as the rest of the world knows him, Tyler "Ty" Burrell. Unfortunately—or fortunately, think Ariel Winter—the discussion on Ty is short. He's an actor. He's good at what he does. He went to college for acting/theater, he obtained an MFA (Masters' of Fine Arts) from Penn State University, he's won Emmys for his work on *Modern Family*, he has a respectable filmography, and he talks to oranges on Tropicana Orange Juice commercials[7]. He's married with an adopted daughter and stays out of the tabloids; respectable, admirable, but fairly boring, much like his father-in-law, Jay Pritchett / Ed O'Neill.

Ed is not a stranger to the role of television patriarch. He was Ed Bundy on *Married...With Children* for 11 seasons. He has been nominated and won many awards and has been a stalwart anchor on these two popular sitcoms, all the while being a cantankerous, shoot-from-the-hip, out of touch but true-to-himself kind of guy. Even though his character is more successful as a businessman on *Modern Family*, in both cases he contributes to the family success by working mundane jobs. His closet business just happens to be more successful than being a shoe salesman on *Married... With Children*. That's his onscreen persona; what about the Real Ed?

Much like Phil/Ty, Ed has enjoyed a successful, boring life as an actor. No scandals, revealing video tapes, or titillating affairs. After receiving his degree in history, he taught social studies at Ursuline High School. His brief stint with the Pittsburgh Steelers (he was cut in training camp) gave him an "in" with Terry Bradshaw, who's appeared on shows with Ed, but didn't earn him a place in NFL Big Time. Ed has been quoted as saying that after his children, earning his black belt in Martial Arts is his single greatest accomplishment[8].

Let's applaud the men and move on to more interesting subject matter. What could be more interesting than beautiful women in a catfight could? Yes, it's time to discuss Gloria and Claire off-screen...

Sofia Vergara (Gloria), has soared to stardom with her role on *Modern Family*. Originally from Colombia, she's the epitome of immigration success as the top paid television actress in 2012-2013. She's appeared in movies (*Chasing Papi, Madea Goes to Jail, Machete Kills, Smurfs,* and others), hosted Spanish-based television programs, and appeared in commercials for Pepsi, Xfinity, State Farm, and CoverGirl. In addition to succeeding on the small and big screens, she's a cancer survivor and has a son, Manolo [9]. On *Modern Family*, she has a son, Manny, an older husband, Jay, and stepchildren, Mitchell and Claire. Mitchell embraces her as a mother figure, chatting over coffee, while Claire is not that crazy about her either as a mother, a wife to her father, or as a friend. How does this translate from real life?

Julie Bowen (Claire) is from Baltimore, MD and has had a successful acting career. Movies (*Happy Gilmore, Multiplicity, Horrible Bosses* and others), television series (*Ed, Lost, Boston Legal, Weeds,* and *Loving*), and endorses Neutrogena products. Due to heart problems, she's had a pacemaker since she was in her twenties. She has three sons, two of which are twins who she was pregnant with at the beginning of season 9 of *Modern Family* [10]. She's beautiful, successful, and overcame serious health issues— on the face of it, Julie and Sofia have a lot in common and should be soul sisters or at least, besties.

This is far, far, FAR from the case. It's time to coin a new term—*worsties*.

Off the *Modern Family* set, their relationship festered over jealousy and erupted on talk shows, specifically *Chelsea Lately*. It began with Sofia accusing Julie of being jealous of her (Sofia's) accent and calling Julie by the wrong last name. In a subsequent show—when asked how it's possible for a co-star to not remember her name—Julie responded in like fashion.

I have never had the chance to fly Sofia [in a] private [jet] and give her jewelry, so my name has no resonance for her [11].

As the fight progressed, it degenerated into name-calling and personal attacks. Julie referred to Sofia as *cholo Barbie*—'cholo' being a derogatory reference to a Hispanic person—and Sofia called Julie's post-baby body *disgusting*. It's definitely unfortunate that two beautiful, successful women could be at each other's throats. However, it does lend an authenticity to their barbs aimed at each other on screen. It's also definitely not a situation solved in a half-hour and summed up in a heart-warming soliloquy. As to heart-warming, it's time to leave the childish adults and move to the mature child, Lily.

Because of the limits imposed on the time children, particularly babies, can be on-screen, babies are typically played by twins. This way, the film time can be increased while avoiding union and child labor law infractions. Such was the situation with Lily, Cam and Mitchell's adopted daughter. In the beginning, Jaden and Ella Hiller—twins—shared the role. For season 3, Aubrey Anderson, a four-year-old actress, took over. The replacement was made because it was sensed that the younger girls wanted to do something else [12]. Specifically, they would become agitated and unhappy when asked to play their roles [13].

As is typical with this type of abrupt casting change, the viewing audience took it in stride. This is nice, because Aubrey appears to have taken her new career in stride, capturing the hearts of the cast as well as the viewers. What about Jaden and Ella? According to their mother, their latest challenge is learning to swim—without lights, cameras or crews.

Discussing Lily/Aubrey brings us to her television daddies, Cam and Mitchell, or Eric Stonestreet and Jesse Tyler Ferguson. Cam/Eric is from Kansas City, KS, trained as a clown, and has appeared in various crime dramas such as *CSI: Crime Scene Investigation* and *Bones*. In reality, he's straight or, as his co-star Jesse describes him, is *gay-for-pay* [14]. Mitchell/Jesse, in contrast, is truly gay.

Jesse, from Missoula, MT, is an enthusiastic advocate for gay rights and marriage equality. Recently, he married his boyfriend of two years and started a not-for-profit organization in support of the same called *Tie the Knot*. This charity sells bow ties to fund efforts to support equality in marriage for same sex couples [15].

Comparing and contrasting the two men's real lives to their onscreen personae reveals multiple levels. Cam is a trained clown from a relatively agrarian background. Jesse is dedicated to furthering gay rights as a mirror to his onscreen career as an environmental advocate. Cam's straight, Jesse's gay. This reality may contribute to the lack of excessive physical interaction that has come under criticism by LGBT advocates. An argument can be made that, historically, actors who were gay were required to interact with female co-stars—think Rock Hudson.

Let's examine those films. Mostly comedies, there wasn't excessive physical interaction in them, either. Much like the sitcoms, passionate embraces and long steamy kisses slow down comedic action plus, it's laudable that society is moving towards more openness with sexual preference and this can be respected in scripts. Regardless of whether or not this is considered in the script writing, the chemistry between the two actors works. Cam has been nominated for and won several Emmys, Golden Globe Awards and various other recognitions. Jesse has received nominations for Emmys and is well-respected on the small screen and stage. How the awards committees and the courtroom of public opinion will view the wedding that ended season 5 will be interesting to watch.

9 So Long, Farewell...

Oscar Hammerstein II / Richard Rodgers
The Sound of Music, 1965

Modern Family is a complex sitcom that coats trendy social issues with an easy to digest coating of laughter and love.   Gay marriage, foreign immigrants, teenage drinking—nothing is off limits, but everything is treated with respect. In the words of Dylan, the family—Hayley, especially—has this *"...killer confidence that's accepting of hot foreigners, gay dudes, and nutty people."*

True to life, however, every topic isn't always tolerated and embraced.   Sometimes they are rejected, similar to how many of the viewers are thinking but don't know how to express in a way that doesn't come across as 'hating.' This realism resonates with a broad demographic and is made even more believable by the challenges that abound in the lives of the actors themselves.

Ultimately, the purpose of the show—as is true with any well-written comedy—is to make the audience laugh and suspend unhappiness for a little while.   To this end, *Modern Family* doesn't just succeed; it triumphs.   So take a seat, turn on the show and embrace a truly *Modern Family*.

References

[1]
http://www.hollywoodreporter.com/news/moder
n-family-star-ariel-winter-393482, November 20,
2012

[2] http://www.eonline.com/news/458634/ariel-
winter-s-mom-slams-sexual-abuse-allegations-
accuses-daughter-of-physical-abuse , September
13, 2013

[3]
http://www.imdb.com/name/nm0405103/bio?ref
_=nm_ov_bio_sm

[4]
http://www.nydailynews.com/entertainment/goss
ip/sarah-hyland-allegedly-groped-fan-modern-
family-event-article-1.1621417 KIRTHANA
RAMISETTI, NEW YORK DAILY NEWS,
Published: Thursday, February 20, 2014, 3:06
PM, Updated: Friday, February 21, 2014, 8:53
AM

[5]

https://twitter.com/mattpro13/status/4364646869
97860352

[6] http://en.wikipedia.org/wiki/Nolan_Gould

[7] http://en.wikipedia.org/wiki/Ty_Burrell

[8] http://en.wikipedia.org/wiki/Ed_O'Neill

[9]
http://en.wikipedia.org/wiki/Sof%C3%ADa_Ver
gara

[10] http://en.wikipedia.org/wiki/Julie_Bowen

[11]
http://entertainment.msn.co.nz/blog.aspx?blogent
ryid=1056455&showcomments=true

[12] http://www.hollywoodreporter.com/live-
feed/modern-family-replaces-baby-lily-222692

[13] http://www.imdb.com/name/nm3902146/news

[14] http://en.wikipedia.org/wiki/Eric_Stonestreet

[15]
http://en.wikipedia.org/wiki/Jesse_Tyler_Fergus
on

Quotes and some character descriptions were taken from:

1. IMDB - Modern Family (TV Series, 2009 -) :
   http://www.imdb.com/title/tt1442437/?ref_=nv_s
   r_1
2. ABC – Modern Family Wiki :
   http://modernfamily.wikia.com/wiki/Modern_Fa
   mily_Wiki
3. http://modernfamilytranscripts.wordpress.com
4. Watching every episode since the pilot ran on
   September 23, 2009.

About the Author

E. Sabbag is a sailor, educator, engineer, and, primarily, a writer. She's a fulltime live-aboard and cruises the world with her husband aboard their ketch-rigged sailboat.

All novels, fiction and non-fiction can be found through her website, **www.TriumphCharters.com**. She writes in several genres, including traditional murder mysteries, paranormal romance, psychological horror and memoirs based on her adventures on and off shore.

This opinion piece is strictly based on her own views after watching the hit sitcom *Modern Family*. This work does not represent the views and opinions of the producers, actors, writers, or networks involved in the creation, production, and distribution of the sitcom. As such, no endorsement is implied from these entities.